the unofficial elf cookbook

the unofficial elf cookbook

From Buddy's Breakfast Spaghetti
to the "World's Best Cup of Coffee,"
Tasty Treats Inspired by a Holiday Classic

bryton taylor

ADAMS MEDIA
NEW YORK LONDON TORONTO SYDNEY NEW DELHI

dedication

To those who carry childlike joy and wonder in their lives, not just at Christmas but all year round, this book is for you. I hope these recipes sprinkle elfish magic, inspiring sweet adventures with friends and family in every season!

Adams Media
An Imprint of Simon & Schuster, LLC
100 Technology Center Drive
Stoughton, Massachusetts 02072

Copyright © 2024 by Simon & Schuster, LLC.

First Adams Media hardcover edition September 2024

ADAMS MEDIA and colophon are registered trademarks of Simon & Schuster, LLC.

Simon & Schuster: Celebrating 100 Years of Publishing in 2024

For information about special discounts for bulk purchases, please contact Simon & Schuster Special Sales at 1-866-506-1949 or business@simonandschuster.com.

The Simon & Schuster Speakers Bureau can bring authors to your live event. For more information or to book an event, contact the Simon & Schuster Speakers Bureau at 1-866-248-3049 or visit our website at www .simonspeakers.com.

Interior design by Kellie Emery
Photographs by Nathan Rega, Harper Point Photography
Food stylist: Kira Friedman
Chefs: Martine English, Christine Tarango, Kira Friedman
Interior images © 123RF/mansum007, helfei; Adobe Stock

Manufactured in the United States of America

1 2024

Library of Congress Cataloging-in-Publication Data
Names: Taylor, Bryton, author.
Title: The unofficial elf cookbook / Bryton Taylor.
Description: First Adams Media hardcover edition. | Stoughton, Massachusetts: Adams Media, 2024. | Series: Unofficial cookbook gift series | Includes index.
Identifiers: LCCN 2024015061 | ISBN 9781507222553 (hc) | ISBN 9781507222560 (ebook)
Subjects: LCSH: Christmas cooking. | Holiday cooking. | Elves--Miscellanea. | LCGFT: Cookbooks.
Classification: LCC TX739.2.C45 T38 2024 | DDC 641.5/686--dc23/eng/20240429
LC record available at https://lccn.loc.gov/2024015061

ISBN 978-1-5072-2255-3
ISBN 978-1-5072-2256-0 (ebook)

contents

acknowledgments

What better way to embrace the Christmas spirit than by writing a Christmas cookbook! While *The Unofficial Home Alone Cookbook* took us on a nostalgic trip to a '90s childhood, *The Unofficial Elf Cookbook* is a whimsical journey to the North Pole, channeling Buddy's boundless enthusiasm for Christmas.

As always, a heartfelt thank-you to the Adams Media team. I've learned that the joy you find in your work is greatly influenced by the people around you. Writing this second cookbook with all of you has been just as wonderful as the first time.

Special thanks to Julia for her patience, especially when my creativity panicked. Your calm reassurance and guidance were exactly what I needed!

Handing over raw creative work can be daunting, no matter how objective you try to remain or how much you try to polish your work. Sarah, knowing you were the person on the other side to catch the words and recipes made this so much easier! As always, you brought it all together. And thank you to Jamie for being our second set of eyes to bring consistency and polish to the book.

We judge a book by its cover and eat with our eyes, so immense gratitude is due to Erin, Lisa, Julia, Kellie, and Harper Point Photography. The attention to detail that brought each scene alive was noted by many readers of *The Unofficial Home Alone Cookbook*, and I know that every reader will be just as captivated by the visuals in this cookbook.

Writing this cookbook truly kicked off the Christmas season, complete with Christmas Spirit Clausometers and Central Park Caroling Coolers. Special thanks to Ron, Madi, Scott, Holly, and Jess—not just for the fun cocktail sessions but for the brainstorming that helped shape this book.

Jess, a special thank-you for helping capture the playful childhood sweetness in Sticky Sidewalks and Swirly Twirly Gumdrop. Dale, thank you for insisting that the Old Saint Nick could only be an old-fashioned cocktail.

Heartfelt thanks to Madi and James, overseen by Skye, who explored a smorgasbord of flavors in muffin tins during midweek dinners, helping me select the combination of tastes that fill this book.

And thank you Mom and Dad, who taught me a secret when I was a little girl: The true magic of Christmas isn't wrapped in shiny paper, nestled under the tree, but is found in qualities that live within us all. It's through our actions that we bring this magic to life, inspiring others to continue to believe.

introduction

Once upon a time, in a magical place far, far away, a human grew to learn the true meaning of Christmas. Traveling through gumdrop seas and the Lincoln Tunnel, he shared that joy and wonder with family, grumpy racoons, and overworked toy store employees. But you don't have to be raised as an elf to understand these holiday essentials...

With *The Unofficial Elf Cookbook*, you can adopt the same Christmas spirit and spread a bit of cheer to those around you—right in your own kitchen! Unlock delicious magic with seventy-five elf-approved recipes straight from the beloved classic. Each dish is either a re-creation of a treat seen in the movie itself or inspired by Buddy, his enchanted upbringing at the North Pole, and his adventures in New York City. As you turn the pages, you'll be able to:

* Treat every day like Christmas by starting off with a breakfast of Arctic Puffin Pancakes or Candy Cane Forest French Toast.
* Avoid midday crashes after a morning of snowy fun with Tickle Fight Tortellini or Boardroom Tussle Tac-Ohs.
* Prepare bite-sized snacks in advance to welcome guests that pop up with Little Buddy's Chex Mix or Son of a Nut-Crackle.
* Find a place for everyone on the dinner list by serving up Christmas-Gram Cannelloni or Nice List Nut Loaf.
* Spread Christmas cheer with mouthwatering desserts like Sugarplum Spread or Milk and Cookies Crumble Cake.
* Help spirits soar to new heights with festive drinks like the Christmas Spirit Clausometers or Elves' Merrymaking Milk Shots.

Just be sure to bring your appetite along for the ride as you set off on this scrumptious journey through forests of bright red and white candy canes, bustling mailrooms brimming with letters and wrapped packages, and more. As you unwrap the joy of the season with *The Unofficial Elf Cookbook*, let it be a reminder that sweetness and cheer are within us all. Now let's turn the page...your own *Elf*-inspired adventures are just beginning!

CHAPTER 1

breakfast

Being an elf means treating every day like Christmas, and what better way to practice this skill than with breakfast each morning! In this chapter, you'll find everything you need to begin the day with a jolly stomach.

Serve up towering stacks of Arctic Puffin Pancakes to share with friends. Whipped up with nougat cream and topped with "snow berries," this recipe is the perfect meal to enjoy before you venture into the snowy wonderland waiting outside. And if your journey is a bit longer, perhaps venturing into the city for some Christmas shopping, sift your way through layers of Candy Cane Forest French Toast to keep you satiated. Gearing up for Santa's big visit? The Big Dance Breakfast Board awaits with an assembly line of ingredients that will have everyone brimming with excitement. To test how well you've mastered your elf lessons, you will want to try Buddy's Breakfast Spaghetti at least once! Candy, chocolate, and maple syrup all in one dish, it effortlessly checks off most of the elves' four food groups. When you follow these simple lessons from the North Pole, breakfast will leave you full and ready to embrace the Christmas spirit throughout the season.

Buddy's Breakfast Spaghetti

Brimming with enthusiasm, Buddy sweetly showers his spaghetti with generosity. A sprinkling of Sno-Caps, a scattering of M&M's, and a dash of mini marshmallows are playful reminders that joy can be rediscovered in the smallest things. Overturn usual breakfast rules and invite your family to make this their own! Decorate the family breakfast table with bowls of chocolate-based candies, topped with a generous swirl of homemade chocolate fudge sauce. To those who still hold a spark of childlike wonder in their heart, this dish is nothing short of a well-balanced, elf-approved breakfast.

SERVES 4

FOR FUDGE SAUCE
1/4 cup unsalted butter
2 tablespoons gently packed light brown sugar
2 tablespoons granulated sugar
1 tablespoon molasses
1 tablespoon cocoa powder
1/2 cup heavy cream
1/2 teaspoon vanilla extract

FOR SPAGHETTI
4 ounces uncooked spaghetti
1/3 cup maple syrup
1/2 cup Fudge Sauce
1/4 cup milk chocolate M&M's
1/4 cup mini marshmallows
1/4 cup Sno-Caps
1 frosted chocolate fudge Pop-Tart, toasted

1. **To make Fudge Sauce:** Melt butter in a medium saucepan over low heat. Add brown sugar, granulated sugar, and molasses and stir until dissolved. Sift in cocoa powder and stir until combined.

2. Pour in heavy cream and bring mixture to a simmer over low heat, stirring occasionally, 5 minutes.

3. Remove pan from heat and stir in vanilla. Let mixture cool 10 minutes before transferring to a medium glass measuring cup. Refrigerate 30 minutes before using. Leftover Fudge Sauce can be stored in an airtight container in refrigerator up to 2 weeks.

4. **To make Spaghetti:** Bring a large pot of salted water to a boil over high heat. Cook spaghetti according to package instructions.

5. Drain spaghetti and divide into four serving bowls.

6. Drizzle maple syrup and 1/8 cup Fudge Sauce evenly over each serving and top with M&M's, marshmallows, and Sno-Caps. Break Pop-Tart into small pieces and crumble on top of bowls. Serve.

Arctic Puffin Pancakes

Buddy's friends know that the best winter adventures are those shared in the warm company of friends. When the sparkling snow awaits outside the window, the best adventures begin with a hot breakfast. The only thing that should be feeling chilly is the heavy cream when you whip it into a flurry to swirl atop the towering stack of pancakes. And while "snow berries" might be a rarity in the human world, sugared cranberries offer a sweet and sparkling stand-in in this recipe.

MAKES 12 PANCAKES

FOR SUGARED CRANBERRIES
1 1/2 cups granulated sugar, divided
3/4 cup boiling water
2/3 cup fresh orange juice
1/4 cup fresh lemon juice
1 tablespoon finely minced orange zest
1 teaspoon ground cardamom
1/8 teaspoon ground nutmeg
1 cup fresh cranberries

FOR PANCAKES
1 large egg, room temperature
1/4 cup granulated sugar
2 teaspoons vanilla extract
1 1/2 cups 2% milk
1/2 teaspoon sea salt
1/2 cup vegetable oil, divided
2 cups all-purpose flour
4 teaspoons baking powder
1/4 teaspoon baking soda
1 (13-ounce) can whipped cream
1/3 cup confectioners' sugar

1. **To make Sugared Cranberries:** In a medium saucepan over high heat, stir together 1 cup sugar and boiling water for 1 minute until sugar is dissolved.

2. Add in orange juice, lemon juice, orange zest, cardamom, and nutmeg. Cover, reduce heat to medium, and bring to a simmer.

3. Once simmering, stir in cranberries, reduce heat to medium-high, and simmer 1 minute.

4. Turn off heat and let mixture cool 10 minutes before straining syrup into a glass measuring cup to cool 30 minutes. Syrup can be stored in an airtight container in the refrigerator for 2 weeks and used as a flavoring for soda water to make an easy Christmas drink.

5. Remove cranberries with a slotted spoon onto a baking sheet lined with parchment paper, separating so cranberries don't touch. Dry cranberries for 30 minutes, then roll in remaining 1/2 cup sugar. Transfer back to baking sheet to dry 1 hour. Sugared cranberries will last for 3 days in an airtight container at room temperature.

6. **To make Pancakes:** In the bowl of a stand mixer on medium speed, whisk egg and sugar together, then add vanilla and milk. Continue whisking 1 minute until frothy. Mix in sea salt and 1/4 cup vegetable oil.

7. In a separate large bowl, sift together flour, baking powder, and baking soda.

8. With mixer running on low, add dry mixture into wet ingredients. Mix together until almost smooth; batter should still have some lumps.

continued

continued

9. Heat a 12" nonstick pan over medium heat 3–5 minutes until hot. Lower heat to low-medium. Pour in 1 tablespoon vegetable oil, tilting pan to distribute.

10. Pour ¼ cup batter into pan for each pancake, leaving 1" space between each. Cook 1 minute until bubbles form around outside of pancake and several begin to form in middle. Quickly slide a spatula under pancake to keep spatula from catching and flip pancake over. Cook 1 minute, then slide onto a serving plate. Repeat with remaining batter, adding 1 tablespoon vegetable oil to pan and wiping spatula clean between each pancake. Halfway through cooking, wipe down pan with a paper towel soaked in vegetable oil to clean pan and avoid burnt pancakes.

11. Divide pancakes into stacks on four serving plates (3 pancakes per stack). Top each stack with whipped cream, 5 Sugared Cranberries, and a dusting of confectioners' sugar.

Nougat Cream

Upgrade your usual can of whipped cream for a magical nougat swirl! In the bowl of a stand mixer, whisk together 1⅔ cups heavy cream, 2 teaspoons almond extract, 1 tablespoon honey, and ¾ cup sifted confectioners' sugar on high speed for 3 minutes until the cream forms firm peaks. Cream will last up to 2 days in an airtight container in the refrigerator. Spoon cream into a piping bag to create decorative swirls on your pancake stacks.

Gimbels Gingerbread Granola

Buddy knows that simple materials like paper, gift wrapping, and twinkle lights can turn a regular storefront into a space worthy of a visit from Santa. Following his example, you can use the following recipe to turn basic ingredients like oats, spices, and gingerbread squares into something magical. This granola is the perfect way to make mornings sparkle, and it lasts for up to two weeks (that is, if you can resist it!).

SERVES 4

1/4 batch gingerbread house
   dough (see Hobbs Holiday
   Gingerbread House recipe
   in Chapter 5)
1 1/2 cups chopped pecans
1 1/4 cups chopped walnuts
3 cups old-fashioned rolled oats
1 tablespoon ground ginger
1/2 teaspoon ground black
   pepper
1 teaspoon ground cloves
1 tablespoon ground cinnamon
1 teaspoon sea salt
1/3 cup melted unsalted butter
1/2 cup maple syrup
1 tablespoon molasses
1 teaspoon vanilla extract
1/2 cup white chocolate candy
   melts
1/4 cup Christmas nonpareils

1. Preheat oven to 350°F.
2. Roll out gingerbread dough into an 8" × 6" rectangle on parchment paper and slide onto a baking sheet.
3. Use a pizza cutter to cut the dough into 1/2" strips vertically, then cut strips horizontally to create squares. Gently loosen dough from parchment paper using your fingers.
4. Bake 10 minutes, then use a wooden spoon to gently stir. Bake another 3 minutes. Pieces will be set but not hard and slightly darker in color. Remove from oven and allow to cool 30 minutes.
5. While dough is cooling, in a large bowl, combine pecans, walnuts, rolled oats, ginger, black pepper, cloves, cinnamon, and sea salt. Set aside.
6. In a measuring cup, mix together butter, maple syrup, molasses, and vanilla. Pour wet mixture into dry ingredients and stir until thoroughly coated.
7. Spread granola mixture evenly on a separate baking sheet lined with parchment paper.
8. Bake 25 minutes, stirring halfway through baking. Let cool 10 minutes, then stir in 2 cups gingerbread squares. Set aside.
9. In a small microwave-safe bowl, melt white chocolate 30 seconds on high, stir, then melt a further 30 seconds.
10. Pour and smooth chocolate onto a silicone-lined baking sheet and sprinkle nonpareils on top. Let cool for 30 minutes before snapping into smaller pieces.
11. Allow granola to cool 2 hours before stirring in chocolate bits and storing in an airtight container at room temperature up to 2 weeks.

The Big Dance Breakfast Board

The top job or "big dance" that all elves aspire to is working on the assembly line in Santa's workshop. Here's your chance for the big show! The joy of Christmas morning will unfold as your kitchen is transformed into Santa's workshop and your own little elves bustle about. Set up a production line and let their nimble fingers assemble their very own breakfast creations.

SERVES 12

FOR CHRISTMAS CREAM
1³⁄4 cups heavy cream
³⁄4 cup sifted confectioners' sugar
1 teaspoon vanilla extract
1 teaspoon Chinese 5 spice
   powder

FOR CANDIED BACON
2 (16-ounce) packs sliced bacon
¹⁄2 cup gently packed light brown
   sugar
2 cups maple syrup, divided

FOR ASSEMBLY
1 (24-count) pack frozen
   pancakes
1 (24-count) pack frozen
   mini waffles
1¹⁄2 cups kiwi, chopped into
   ¹⁄2" pieces
1¹⁄2 cups strawberries,
   chopped into ¹⁄2" pieces
¹⁄2 cup crushed nuts
10 candy canes, crushed
¹⁄2 cup mini marshmallows

1. **To make Christmas Cream:** Add cream, confectioners' sugar, vanilla, and Chinese 5 spice powder to a large bowl. Using a stand mixer, whisk on high 3 minutes until mixture forms firm peaks. Spoon into two small serving bowls, cover, and refrigerate until ready to serve, up to 2 days.

2. **To make Candied Bacon:** Preheat oven to 400°F. Line four baking sheets with parchment paper.

3. Arrange bacon evenly on baking sheets, keeping slices from overlapping. Sprinkle brown sugar evenly over bacon, then drizzle 1 cup maple syrup on top.

4. Bake 20 minutes. Remove bacon from oven and let cool 5 minutes to crisp up.

5. **To Assemble:** Heat frozen pancakes and mini waffles according to package instructions.

6. Spoon fruits into piles on one side of a large serving board.

7. Spoon crushed nuts, candy canes, and mini marshmallows into serving bowls of varying sizes. Place bacon strips upright into two tall glasses and pour remaining 1 cup maple syrup into two smaller serving jugs.

8. Add 2 bowls of Christmas Cream to board, and evenly arrange bowls and glasses on serving board. Stack pancakes and waffles in two separate piles around serving containers. Place tongs and small spoons into toppings. Serve.

Candy Cane Forest French Toast

Your family won't need to trek through candy cane forests or gumdrop seas for a magical breakfast! Dusting French toast with snowy slopes of confectioners' sugar and dotting each piece with mini candy canes between meringue trees will bring the magic home. Preparation is always key for a seamless breakfast adventure, so make sure your bread has a dense texture, is cut thick, and is a few days old so it can soak up the custard and make it to the pan without falling apart on the way.

SERVES 4

FOR MERINGUE TREES
2 large egg whites, room temperature
1/2 teaspoon cream of tartar
1/4 teaspoon sea salt
1/2 cup granulated sugar
1/2 teaspoon vanilla extract

FOR FRENCH TOAST
4 large egg yolks, room temperature
3/4 cup 2% milk, room temperature
1/2 cup light cream, room temperature
3/4 cup confectioners' sugar, divided
1 teaspoon sea salt
2 teaspoons vanilla extract
8 (1"-thick) slices stale white bread
1/4 cup unsalted butter, divided
12 mini candy canes
2 teaspoons ground cinnamon
1/2 cup maple syrup

1. **To make Meringue Trees:** Preheat oven to 250°F. Line two baking sheets with parchment paper.

2. In the bowl of a stand mixer, whisk egg whites, cream of tartar, and salt on high speed 1 minute until egg whites start foaming. With mixer still running on high, gradually add sugar 1 tablespoon at a time, waiting 30 seconds before adding more. Continue whisking 3 minutes more until meringue is thick, glossy, and forms firm peaks when mixer is lifted. Whisk in vanilla.

3. Cut a corner off a sandwich bag and insert a 1/2" 8-point drop flower tip, ensuring it is halfway through hole cut in bag. Scoop meringue into bag, then twist open end closed to seal and contain meringue. Gently squeeze to release any air.

4. Pipe meringue onto baking sheets by holding bag directly above sheet. Apply steady pressure for 3 seconds to create the lower tree section, then release. Raise bag slightly higher to create middle tree section, keeping tip touching meringue. Apply pressure for 2 seconds and release again. Raise bag and repeat 1/2 second for tree tip. Repeat to make 11 more Meringue Trees.

5. Lower oven temperature to 195°F and bake Meringue Trees 1 1/2 hours.

6. Turn off oven, keep oven door shut, and allow to cool 2 hours. Meringues will be crisp on the outside and lift off the parchment without sticking. Store Meringue Trees in an airtight container at room temperature until ready to use, up to 2 weeks.

7. **To make French Toast:** Whisk together egg yolks, milk, cream, $1/4$ cup confectioners' sugar, salt, and vanilla in a medium bowl.

8. Lay 1 bread slice in bowl, leave 10 seconds to soak up egg mixture, then flip to coat other side another 10 seconds.

9. In a medium nonstick frying pan, melt $1/2$ tablespoon butter over medium heat. Fry 1 coated bread slice 2 minutes, then flip and fry other side another 2 minutes. Remove to a large plate. Repeat frying with remaining bread slices, adding another $1/2$ tablespoon butter to pan between each slice.

10. Divide French Toast among four serving plates. Top each serving with 3 Meringue Trees and press 3 mini candy canes into French Toast. Sprinkle cinnamon and remaining $1/2$ cup confectioners' sugar over each stack of French Toast. Serve with maple syrup on the side.

Tinker Training Tart

Papa Elf is always on hand to keep Santa's sleigh charged up and soaring. When preparing for your own daily takeoff, breakfast skills are worth developing—and what better place to begin than tinkering around with tarts? This breakfast tart is something you can quickly fix with leftovers from The Big Dance Breakfast Board (see recipe in this chapter), or you can tinker around with what's in your pantry. Whatever you add to this recipe, you'll be ready to power through the morning after filling your own engine.

SERVES 4

1 1/2 tablespoons olive oil
2 (10") puff pastry sheets, defrosted
5 large eggs
1/2 cup 2% milk
3 garlic cloves, crushed
1/2 teaspoon ground cumin
1 teaspoon lemon zest
1 tablespoon lemon juice
3/4 teaspoon sea salt
1/2 teaspoon ground black pepper
4 slices cooked candied bacon, roughly chopped
4 1/4 cups fresh arugula, divided
2 cups freshly grated Cheddar cheese
1/2 cup freshly grated Parmesan cheese

1. Preheat oven to 350°F.
2. Grease a 9" deep-dish pie pan with olive oil and drape one sheet puff pastry over pan. Rotate second sheet puff pastry slightly before draping on top, so edges don't align.
3. Gently press pastry into pan. Pierce pastry evenly with a fork and bake for 10 minutes while mixing filling.
4. In a large mixing bowl, whisk eggs and milk together. Stir in garlic, cumin, lemon zest, lemon juice, salt, black pepper, and bacon.
5. Rinse arugula and dry thoroughly with a tea towel to remove excess moisture. Roughly chop, reserving 1/4 cup, then stir into mixture.
6. Stir in Cheddar and scoop mixture into pie pan on pastry. Sprinkle with Parmesan and bake 40 minutes until center is just set with a slight jiggle but is no longer liquid. Set aside 5 minutes before slicing.
7. Top with remaining 1/4 cup arugula and serve.

North Pole Parfaits

Snowdrifts, snow-capped trees, dancing snowflakes, ice floes, and candy canes swirl together to create the magic of the North Pole—the stage is set for winter wonderland. You'll be setting the perfect scene, too, with this lovely, layered breakfast that will transform your morning and transport your family to a world of whipped enchantment. It's a creation worthy of an elf!

SERVES 8

1 1/2 cups candied cherries
1 cup frozen raspberries
1/4 cup lemon juice
1 tablespoon boiling water
1 1/2 cups vanilla yogurt
4 cups Gimbels Gingerbread
    Granola (see recipe in this
    chapter)
2 tablespoons Christmas
    nonpareils

1. In a blender, purée candied cherries, raspberries, lemon juice, and boiling water.

2. Transfer purée to a small saucepan over high heat and cook 5 minutes until simmering.

3. Reduce heat to low-medium and continue cooking, stirring occasionally, 5 minutes.

4. Turn off heat and allow purée to cool 10 minutes before transferring to a glass airtight container. Refrigerate 30 minutes, up to 3 days.

5. In each of 8 tall glasses, layer 1 tablespoon purée, 1 1/2 tablespoons yogurt, and 1/4 cup Gimbels Gingerbread Granola, reserving a few pieces of white chocolate from granola. Repeat the layers twice more. Top each parfait with remaining pieces of white chocolate and sprinkle with Christmas nonpareils. Serve with parfait spoons.

Cotton-Headed Ninny Muffins

Sometimes, a person's special talents can lie outside of what may be expected. Regardless of whether you are skilled at baking or not, these oat muffins are a cinch to make and won't leave you feeling like a ninny. Every person has their own special way of sprinkling joy, and yours will shine through by topping these muffins with colorful mini meringues. If you really want to make heads turn, top the muffins with a fluffy puff of cotton candy. Watch as every sweet tooth lights up at your charming creation!

MAKES 12 MUFFINS

FOR MINI MERINGUES
2 large egg whites, room temperature
1/2 teaspoon cream of tartar
1/4 teaspoon sea salt
1/2 cup granulated sugar
1/2 teaspoon vanilla extract
1/2 teaspoon blue food coloring
1/2 teaspoon pink food coloring
1/2 teaspoon yellow food coloring

FOR OAT MUFFINS
2 cups all-purpose flour
1 tablespoon baking powder
1/2 teaspoon sea salt
3/4 cup granulated sugar
1 1/2 cups rolled oats
1 large egg, room temperature
1 1/4 cups 2% milk
1/3 cup vegetable oil

1. **To make Mini Meringues:** The night before making Cotton-Headed Ninny Muffins, whisk together a batch of meringues.

2. Preheat oven to 250°F. Line two baking sheets with parchment paper.

3. In the bowl of a stand mixer, whisk egg whites, cream of tartar, and salt on high speed 1 minute until egg whites start foaming.

4. Gradually add sugar, 1 tablespoon at a time, waiting 30 seconds before each addition. Once all sugar is added, continue whisking a further 3 minutes until the meringue is thick, glossy, and forms firm peaks when mixer is lifted. Whisk in vanilla.

5. Separate meringue mixture into three bowls. Whisk different food coloring into each bowl until color has blended through.

6. Cut a corner off a sandwich bag and insert a small drop flower tip, ensuring it is halfway through hole cut in bag. Scoop one color meringue into bag, then twist open end closed to seal and contain meringue. Gently squeeze to release any air.

7. Pipe meringue onto baking sheet by holding bag directly above sheet. Apply steady pressure for 1 second, then release. Continue in rows, making round mini meringues (you should be able to make around 84).

8. Repeat with remaining meringue colors using a clean sandwich bag and washing piping tip between colors.

9. Lower oven temperature to 195°F and bake mini meringues 1 hour.

10. Turn off oven, keep oven door shut, and allow meringues to cool 2 hours. Store in an airtight container at room temperature until ready to use, up to 3 weeks.

11. **To make Oat Muffins:** Preheat oven to 455°F. Line a 12-cup muffin pan with colorful muffin liners.

12. In the bowl of a stand mixer, sift together flour, baking powder, salt, and sugar. Stir in rolled oats until combined.

13. In a separate measuring cup, use a fork to beat egg. Whisk in milk and vegetable oil until the mixture is just blended.

14. Pour wet ingredients into bowl with dry ingredients. Mix on medium speed just until combined. Do not overmix to keep the muffins light and fluffy.

15. Distribute batter evenly among lined muffin pan divots. Press 7 mini meringues on top of each muffin, spacing them out evenly.

16. Bake 5 minutes. Muffin tops will have begun to rise. Reduce oven temperature to 425°F without opening oven door and continue to bake an additional 15 minutes until golden on top and a toothpick inserted in center comes out clean. Allow muffins to cool in pan 10 minutes before serving. Let muffins cool a further 2 hours on a wire rack before storing in an airtight container up to 3 days.

Fluffed-Up Top

The trick to making muffins light and well-rounded is by slipping them into the oven at a hotter temperature for 5 minutes, giving them the time needed to rapidly puff up on top. Then reduce the heat to let the muffins finish baking all the way through without burning.

Toy Tester Tater Tots

When friends pop up during the holiday season, they'll burst with excitement when they find their favorite holiday side dish has been repackaged into bite-sized, festive treats. Be the most organized elf by boxing up these little gems in the freezer, ready to spread cheer whenever the moment arises. These little tater tots dipped in Marshmallow Fluff and rolled in toasted cinnamon crumbs are sure to pass the festive taste test! Just be careful that you don't eat them all before you have the chance to serve them.

MAKES 40 TOTS

- 1 1/2 pounds sweet potato, peeled and cut into even, small chunks
- 1 tablespoon table salt
- 1 teaspoon vanilla extract
- 3 tablespoons unsalted butter
- 1/3 cup all-purpose flour
- 1/2 cup grated Cheddar cheese
- 2 cups panko bread crumbs, toasted and divided
- 3/4 cup gently packed light brown sugar
- 1 1/2 teaspoons cinnamon
- 1/2 cup pulsed pecans
- 1/4 teaspoon sea salt
- 3/4 cup Marshmallow Fluff
- 1 tablespoon heavy cream

1. Preheat oven to 390°F.

2. Place potatoes and table salt in a large pot of cold water. Bring to a boil over high heat and cook 8 minutes. You should be able to use a fork to pierce sweet potatoes easily but will find the center firm.

3. Remove pot from heat, drain, and run under cold water to stop cooking. Set aside for 10 minutes.

4. When cool to touch, place potatoes onto a clean tea towel. Place another tea towel on top and press down to absorb moisture. Set aside.

5. Mix vanilla and butter in a small microwave-safe bowl and melt 20 seconds on high.

6. Stir butter mixture into sweet potato, then add flour, grated cheese, and 1/2 cup bread crumbs and stir to combine.

7. Scoop 1 tablespoon sweet potato mixture and form into a nugget shape. Roll in 1/2 cup bread crumbs before placing on an unlined baking sheet. Repeat with remaining potato mixture. Bake 20 minutes.

8. For Cinnamon Toast Crumbs: Stir together brown sugar, cinnamon, pecans, sea salt, and remaining 1 cup toasted bread crumbs in a medium bowl. Set aside.

9. For Marshmallow Dip: Pour Marshmallow Fluff and cream into a medium glass microwave-safe bowl. Microwave 45 seconds at 50 percent power. Stir until marshmallows and cream are incorporated.

10. Serve Tater Tots on a large plate with skewers to allow for dipping in Marshmallow Dip and Cinnamon Toast Crumbs.

Leon's Lemon Drizzle Snowdrifts

Leon has seen the world and is happy to roll out some cool advice to Buddy. And if visitors roll up to your door one day, you'll have something cool to serve up yourself. Whisk together Snowdrifts the night before, and you'll be all set to serve them up when the sun rises. Every morning is a golden opportunity to make your day glisten when it's topped with lemon meringue drizzle and dusted with a snowy blanket of coconut flakes. Even if the weather outside is frightful, invite friends in and enjoy a scoop of Leon's Lemon Drizzle Snowdrifts. They're delightful!

SERVES 4

FOR LEMON MERINGUE SAUCE

1/4 cup lemon juice
1 teaspoon lemon zest, finely chopped
1/4 cup granulated sugar
2 tablespoons water
2 large egg yolks
2 tablespoons unsalted butter
2 tablespoons Marshmallow Fluff
1/4 teaspoon yellow food coloring

FOR SNOWDRIFTS

1 1/2 cups plain Greek yogurt
3/4 cup heavy coconut cream
3/4 teaspoon vanilla extract
3/4 cup confectioners' sugar
3/4 cup desiccated coconut
6 teaspoons shredded coconut flakes

1. **To make Lemon Meringue Sauce:** In a medium saucepan, combine lemon juice, lemon zest, sugar, and water. Heat over medium heat while stirring until sugar dissolves completely.

2. In a separate small bowl, whisk egg yolks. Gradually pour 2 tablespoons hot lemon mixture into egg yolks and whisk to temper eggs.

3. Slowly pour tempered egg mixture back into saucepan, whisking constantly. Continue to cook the mixture over medium heat 5 minutes, stirring frequently.

4. Remove from heat and stir in butter, Marshmallow Fluff, and yellow food coloring until fully incorporated.

5. Allow sauce to sit 10 minutes before pouring into an airtight glass container. Refrigerate 1 hour up to 3 days until ready to use.

6. **To make Snowdrifts:** In the bowl of a stand mixer, add yogurt, coconut cream, vanilla, and confectioners' sugar. Whisk ingredients together on medium speed 5 minutes until thick and stiff. Gently fold in desiccated coconut until evenly distributed.

7. Scoop mixture into an airtight container. Refrigerate 2 hours up to overnight.

8. To assemble, scoop Snowdrift mixture into four serving bowls, drizzle 1 tablespoon Lemon Meringue Sauce on top of each bowl and top each bowl with 1 1/2 teaspoons shredded coconut. Serve remaining Lemon Meringue Sauce on the side.

Favorite Smiley Potatoes

Smiling is one of Buddy's favorite things to do—and everyone will be smiling when they dig into these grin-inducing hash browns. Drizzle ribbons of sriracha ketchup on the side to really light up the plate and serve alongside eggs and bacon. This recipe generously exceeds the usual serving for four, making sure there's a surplus of smiles in the refrigerator for those mornings when you need to grin and go. Heat leftovers in the microwave for 30 seconds on high before serving to have everyone beaming from ear to ear.

SERVES 7 (MAKES 14 SMILEYS)

2 pounds russet potatoes
1/3 cup panko bread crumbs, toasted
1/2 teaspoon sea salt
2 tablespoons cornstarch
1/2 cup vegetable oil
1/3 cup sriracha ketchup

1. Preheat oven to 425°F.

2. Pierce potatoes with a fork, place in a large saucepan over medium heat, and cover with water. Bring to a boil and cook 15 minutes until potatoes are tender but still firm near center when pierced with a fork.

3. Remove from heat, drain, and immerse in cold water. Refrigerate 5 minutes to cool. Peel and grate.

4. In a small bowl, mix bread crumbs, salt, and cornstarch. Add to potatoes and combine.

5. On a floured surface, press potato mixture into a 1/2"-thick layer. Cut out 14 circles using a 3" cookie cutter. Use a straw to cut out eyes and a spoon to carve a mouth.

6. Place Smileys on a parchment paper–lined baking sheet. Drizzle each with 1/2 tablespoon vegetable oil. Bake 40 minutes until golden brown. To serve, divide Smileys evenly, and add a side of sriracha ketchup to each plate.

7. Cool leftovers 30 minutes, then store in an airtight container in refrigerator up to 3 days.

Rockefeller Cinnamon Raisin Rolls

Beneath the shimmering twinkle of the Rockefeller Center Christmas Tree, Buddy and Jovie circle around the rink, hand in hand. In a similar embrace, these rolls will be ready to cozy up under the oven's warmth after the dough is prepped the night before and allowed to rise overnight.

MAKES 12 ROLLS

FOR DOUGH

4 cups bread flour
1 teaspoon sea salt
1 ($^{1}/_{4}$-ounce) packet active dry yeast
$^{1}/_{4}$ cup granulated sugar
$^{1}/_{4}$ cup unsalted butter, room temperature
2 large eggs, room temperature
1 (12-ounce) can evaporated milk
$^{1}/_{2}$ cup unsalted butter, softened
1 cup heavy cream, room temperature

FOR CINNAMON RAISIN FILLING

$^{1}/_{2}$ cup gently packed light brown sugar
2 tablespoons ground cinnamon
$^{1}/_{2}$ teaspoon sea salt
1 cup raisins

FOR GLAZE

2 cups confectioners' sugar
3 tablespoons 2% milk
1 teaspoon vanilla extract

1. **To make Dough:** In the large bowl of a stand mixer, use the dough hook attachment to combine bread flour, salt, yeast, and sugar. Add $^{1}/_{4}$ cup butter, eggs, and evaporated milk. Mix on medium speed 5 minutes until smooth. Halfway through, use a spatula to scrape dough from sides of bowl.

2. Form dough into a ball, place in a large oiled bowl, and lightly coat dough with oil. Cover bowl with plastic wrap and refrigerate 8 hours up to overnight to rise.

3. When ready to bake, dust a surface with flour. Place dough on surface and let sit 15 minutes.

4. Roll dough into a 9" × 15" rectangle. Spread $^{1}/_{2}$ cup softened butter on dough.

5. **To make Cinnamon Raisin Filling:** Mix brown sugar, cinnamon and salt together, then sprinkle over butter on Dough and sprinkle raisins on top.

6. To assemble, roll dough from long side into a tube shape. Cut into twelve 1 $^{1}/_{4}$"-thick slices using a bread knife.

7. Line a 14" roasting pan with parchment paper. Place dough slices in pan, cut side up, with $^{1}/_{2}$" space between each roll. Cover with a tea towel and let sit 20 minutes.

8. Preheat oven to 350°F. Pour heavy cream over rolls. Cover again and let sit 20 minutes.

9. Remove tea towel and bake on lower rack of oven 25 minutes. Rolls are done when firm but spring back when pressed lightly. Allow to cool 10 minutes in pan.

10. **To make Glaze:** Whisk confectioners' sugar, milk, and vanilla together in a small bowl 1 minute until smooth, then pour over rolls.

11. Serve, or refrigerate in an airtight container up to 2 days. Reheat in microwave 45 seconds at 50 percent power before serving.

CHAPTER 2

lunch

Time flies when you've spent the morning frolicking and playing, making the most of a freshly laid blanket of snow. And before you know it, your stomach is rumbling, reminding you to refuel for more festive fun. This is where a merry lunch comes in! The following chapter is full of delicious and easy-to-make recipes so you can get back to snow angels and snuggles in no time.

Nimbly sidestep midday energy crashes with Yellow Cab Polenta Medallions, keeping your holiday spirits and taste buds revved up with the seasonal flavors of rosemary and cranberry. Make lunchtime a smooth sleighride by preparing in advance. Whip up a savory and sweet pasta sauce for a shared family lunch, infusing it with joyful memories (and a dash of maple syrup!) in the Swirly Twirly Spaghetti. Or roll up your Favorite Color Rolls before you head out in the morning so you can quickly tumble back into the snow after lunch. And when your crowd resembles Santa's list—ever-growing—keep the zesty exchanges under wraps by serving up a large batch of Boardroom Tussle Tac-Ohs. Everyone will be charging back for seconds before they dash back out for more winter activities.

Favorite Color Rolls

It is hardly a surprise that Buddy, always eager to welcome everyone warmly and ever the ray of sunshine, answers the phone with cheerful enthusiasm. There's no need to ask what everyone's favorite color is when you serve up these bright vegetable rolls! To keep the rice paper rolls bursting with freshness, though, you can get everyone involved in the fun. Prepare the kaleidoscope of vibrant vegetables ahead of time, then gather everyone around to wrap up their favorite hues.

SERVES 5

3.5 ounces dried vermicelli rice noodles
1/2 teaspoon turmeric powder
3 cups boiling water
10 (8 1/2") round rice paper sheets
1/4 cup fresh mint leaves
1 large carrot, julienned
1 large cucumber, julienned
1 large green onion, julienned
1 large yellow bell pepper, seeded, cored, and thinly sliced
1 large red bell pepper, seeded, cored, and thinly sliced
1/2 cup Thai sweet chili sauce

1. In a large 4-cup measuring glass, add vermicelli noodles and turmeric powder. Pour boiling water over noodles to cover completely. Stir to dissolve turmeric. Let sit 5 minutes until noodles are soft, then drain.

2. Fill a 9" pie plate with very warm water (should be bearable to touch).

3. Submerge 1 rice paper sheet in water 5 seconds to soften.

4. Lay softened sheet on a silicone mat and smooth out creases. Place 3 mint leaves in center of rice paper. Add 1/10 drained noodles to paper over mint in a 5" × 1 1/2" line, leaving a 1" gap at top and bottom. Add 3 carrot sticks, 2 cucumber strips, 2 pieces green onion, and 2 slices each yellow and red bell pepper on top of noodles.

5. Fold bottom of rice paper up, then fold right side over fillings. To keep filings tight in the sheet, use your hand to drag sheet with fillings back toward righthand side. Fold top edge over, then roll toward left side to close. Repeat steps 3–5 with remaining ingredients to make 10 rolls.

6. Slice each roll in half and stand upright on a large serving plate. Serve with Thai sweet chili sauce on the side for dipping.

7. If making 3 or more hours in advance, cover rolls with a damp tea towel and refrigerate in an airtight container to prevent drying out.

Empire Button Bagel Bites

Buddy pushes everyone's buttons no matter where he goes! Fortunately, these little bagel bites will be pushing all the right ones come lunchtime, especially when you find yourself with a surplus of egg yolks after some festive baking. Whether icing your Hobbs Holiday Gingerbread House or shaking up Swirly Twirly Gumdrops, some recipes in this book only need egg whites. Use the remaining egg yolks to lift your lunch game to new heights! Ready in minutes and served on a layer of baby spinach, these bagel bites will ascend straight to the top of your list of lunch favorites.

SERVES 4

2 plain bagels
6 (7½"-long) slices bacon
3 tablespoons Dijon mustard
¼ cup Kewpie mayonnaise
¼ cup water
12 large egg yolks

1. Slice and toast each bagel 2 minutes until golden brown. Cut each half into three sections.

2. Line a microwave-proof baking dish with two layers of paper towels and top with a sheet of parchment paper. Arrange bacon slices in a single layer on parchment. If the bacon pieces are too long, cut to fit and prevent overlapping. Cover bacon completely with another sheet of parchment paper. Microwave 4 minutes on high.

3. Dab bacon with paper towels to remove excess oil and cut slices to fit on top of each bagel section.

4. Stir together Dijon mustard and Kewpie mayonnaise in a small bowl and add 1 teaspoon on top of each bacon slice.

5. Fill a wide soup bowl with a flat bottom.

6. Over a medium bowl, crack an egg and separate yolk from the white by letting whites slip through your fingers, keeping yolk intact.

7. Gently place yolks into soup bowl and microwave 25 seconds on high. Place an egg yolk on each bagel section.

8. Divide 3 Bagel Bites each onto four serving plates.

Swirly Twirly Spaghetti

Time spent with family can be a little sticky. But it's nothing you can't handle when you have a simple from-scratch pasta sauce recipe and a bottle of maple syrup up your sleeve. Lunch will become all the more sweeter, as maple syrup simply enhances the natural sweetness of the tomatoes. Give this easy recipe a whirl!

SERVES 4

10 cups large Roma tomatoes, cut into wedges

2 cups yellow onion, sliced into strips

3 tablespoons crushed fresh garlic

¼ cup maple syrup

1 cup olive oil

2 teaspoons sea salt

1 teaspoon smoked paprika

1 teaspoon ground black pepper

8 ounces uncooked spaghetti

1. Preheat oven to 400°F.

2. Scatter tomatoes evenly over a large, unlined baking sheet and evenly distribute onion and garlic on top. Drizzle maple syrup and olive oil evenly over vegetables, then sprinkle with salt, smoked paprika, and black pepper.

3. Bake vegetables 55 minutes until tomatoes are wrinkly, then let cool in pan 15 minutes.

4. Cook spaghetti according to package instructions. Drain and divide into four serving bowls or plates.

5. Transfer tomato mixture to a blender and purée until smooth. Divide over spaghetti. Leftover sauce can be refrigerated in an airtight container up to 5 days.

Ready Spaghetti

Want to upgrade a jar of tomato sauce instead of using Roma tomatoes? Roast 2 cups sliced yellow onions and 3 tablespoons minced garlic with ⅓ cup olive oil drizzled on top for 45 minutes, stirring halfway through. Purée with 2 teaspoons salt, 1 teaspoon smoked paprika, and 1 teaspoon black pepper. Add to a medium saucepan over medium heat and stir in a 24-ounce jar of tomato sauce. Heat 5 minutes before pouring over cooked spaghetti.

Winter Walrus Waffle Cones

It's a whimsical world to be raised in when walruses wave you off on frosty adventures and icebergs are your playground. Skate back to your own childhood days with a playful spin on the classic PB&J. In this recipe, creamy ricotta keeps the texture of the peanut butter light, and jelly is swapped for a burst of fresh strawberries. Served in crispy waffle cones, grab a few before sailing off on your next expedition for the day!

SERVES 4

1 cup ricotta cheese
6 tablespoons creamy peanut butter
¼ cup honey
4 single-serve waffle cones
8 teaspoons crushed unsalted peanuts, divided
6 large fresh strawberries, hulled and chopped into quarters

1. In the bowl of a stand mixer, whip ricotta, peanut butter, and honey together until smooth and combined.

2. Scoop 1 tablespoon ricotta mixture into each waffle cone. Spread ricotta around inside of cone, coating sides evenly.

3. Sprinkle 1 teaspoon crushed nuts over ricotta. Scoop an additional 1 tablespoon ricotta mixture on top of each cone and sprinkle another 1 teaspoon crushed nuts over top to finish. Place 1 tablespoon strawberries around inner edge of each cone. Serve.

Scramble and Crunch

For a savory twist, pack waffle cones with fluffy scrambled eggs and crispy bacon from the Empire Button Bagel Bites (see recipe in this chapter). In place of crispy bacon, you can use candied bacon from The Big Dance Breakfast Board (Chapter 1).

Central Park Rangers Reubens

Anything other than the trio of corned beef, Russian dressing, and sauerkraut on rye might seem controversial for a Reuben, but there's no need to take things so seriously. Lighten things up with a dash of holiday spirit using a cranberry-spiced dressing. The only thing you'll need to contain are the festive flavors, but don't worry: A sturdy rye bread will help you rein it all in. Don't forget to hitch a side of potato chips to your plate!

SERVES 4

¼ cup Kewpie mayonnaise
1 tablespoon Dijon mustard
¼ cup cranberry sauce
½ teaspoon allspice
½ teaspoon ground cinnamon
1 tablespoon horseradish cream
16 slices corned beef
9 tablespoons unsalted
    butter, divided (at room
    temperature)
1⅓ cups sauerkraut
8 slices rye bread
16 slices Swiss cheese

1. In a small bowl, stir together Kewpie mayonnaise, Dijon mustard, cranberry sauce, allspice, cinnamon, and horseradish cream until combined. Refrigerate 30 minutes to allow flavors to infuse.

2. In a large frying pan, heat ¼ cup water for 1 minute. Add corned beef slices and cover with a lid slightly smaller than pan. Over medium heat, warm meat 1 minute.

3. Push corned beef to one side of pan. Melt 3 tablespoons butter 30 seconds in empty section of pan. Squeeze out excess moisture from sauerkraut, add to pan, and stir-fry in butter 1 minute.

4. Butter each slice of bread with remaining 6 tablespoons butter, placing bread buttered side down on a large cutting board (these will be the outsides of the sandwich).

5. Spread dressing on the unbuttered side of each slice of bread.

6. On half of the bread slices, layer 2 slices Swiss, 4 slices corned beef, sauerkraut, and 2 more slices Swiss. Top with remaining bread slices to form sandwiches.

7. Place sandwiches in pan and cook over high heat 2 minutes. Use a smaller lid to press down on sandwiches. Flip and cook an additional 2 minutes, still covered with smaller lid, until golden brown. Cut in half and serve.

Publisher's Pressed Paninis

When the pressure piles up, Walter knows all you can do is press on! As you get swept up in navigating the bustling holiday season, take a page out of Walter's book by whipping up these paninis. While the cheese merrily melts into the prosciutto and fig jam, the Chestnut and Sage Pesto adds a dash of Christmas flavor. You'll never be short on lunch ideas with a double batch on hand, making sure that no matter how packed the days get, there will always be a taste of Christmas waiting. Serve with a mixed green salad drizzled with honey Dijon vinaigrette on the side.

SERVES 4

FOR CHESTNUT AND SAGE PESTO

1 tablespoon unsalted butter
$1/2$ tablespoon minced garlic
$1/4$ cup fresh sage leaves
2 ounces peeled and cooked chestnuts, chopped
$1/4$ cup freshly grated Parmesan cheese
$1/4$ teaspoon chicken bouillon powder
$1/4$ cup olive oil

FOR ASSEMBLY

$1/4$ cup olive oil
4 (9") ciabatta rolls, halved
$1/2$ cup Chestnut and Sage Pesto
$1/2$ cup fig jam
24 slices prosciutto
16 slices provolone cheese

1. **To make Chestnut and Sage Pesto:** Melt butter in a medium frying pan over medium heat 30 seconds. Add garlic and sage and cook 4 minutes, stirring continuously.

2. Add chestnuts and cook 8 minutes, stirring occasionally, then remove from heat and allow mixture to cool in pan 5 minutes.

3. Transfer to a food processor and add Parmesan and chicken bouillon powder. Run food processor while gradually pouring in olive oil until mixture is fully processed.

4. **To Assemble:** Preheat panini press.

5. Drizzle olive oil on insides of ciabatta rolls. Place bread on panini press, oiled side down and lid open. (You may need to trim ends of sandwich before placing in press, depending on size of press.) Cook 2 minutes to warm, then remove from heat.

6. Spread 2 tablespoons Pesto on half of each roll and 2 tablespoons fig jam on other half. Layer 6 slices prosciutto and 4 slices provolone on Pesto. Close paninis and place in press another 3 minutes. Serve. Leftover Pesto can be stored in an airtight container in the refrigerator for up to 1 week.

Yellow Cab Polenta Medallions

When you've spent the morning zooming around like an elf in New York City, you might not be paying attention to your fuel levels. To dodge the midday crash when you arrive back home, whip up this satisfying polenta the night before so you can enjoy these sizzling medallions before your energy screeches to a halt. Christmas stuffing flavors collide with warmed walnuts, rosemary, and a burst of tart cranberry on top of these golden ornaments.

SERVES 4

5 cups chicken stock
2 cups polenta
5 tablespoons olive oil, divided
1 teaspoon minced fresh garlic
1 tablespoon finely chopped fresh rosemary leaves
1 cup walnuts, chopped
3/4 cup cranberry sauce
4 cups fresh arugula leaves, washed
1 Barlett or Anjou pear, cored and finely sliced
1/2 cup vinaigrette dressing

1. In a large saucepan over medium heat, bring chicken stock to a rolling boil. Slowly pour in polenta, stirring with a wooden spoon until combined.

2. Reduce heat to low. Cook 20 minutes, stirring every few minutes, until polenta mixture thickens.

3. Line a 9" × 9" casserole dish with parchment paper. Pour polenta into dish and cover with another layer of parchment paper to smooth top. Refrigerate 2 hours up to overnight.

4. Remove top parchment paper and use a 2 1/2" round cookie cutter to cut out 12 circles of polenta.

5. Heat a large frying pan over medium heat. Pour in 2 tablespoons olive oil and heat 1 minute before adding garlic, rosemary, and walnuts. Stir until walnuts are coated in oil and let cook 2 minutes.

6. Transfer nuts to a medium bowl and set aside.

7. Pour remaining 3 tablespoons olive oil into same large pan and add polenta circles to pan in a single layer, cooking in batches as needed.

8. Use a spatula to continuously push polenta around pan during first 1 minute of cooking to prevent sticking.

9. Fry polenta 3 minutes more, flip, and cook an additional 3 minutes.

10. Place three polenta circles each onto four serving plates. Top each piece with 1 tablespoon cranberry sauce and 1 teaspoon nuts.

11. Divide arugula leaves and sliced pear evenly on the side of medallions and drizzle arugula and pear with vinaigrette dressing. Serve.

Snuggled-Up Ham and Cheese Dough Scrolls

A holiday to-do list isn't complete without a good old-fashioned snuggle. And when you wrap ham with rich tomato and sharp cheese in a delicious soft dough, everyone will be looking forward to embracing lunchtime. Like a hug, these are best served warm. When you're ready to tuck into leftovers, a quick zap in the microwave for 15 seconds rekindles their coziness.

MAKES 15

1 batch Rockefeller Cinnamon Raisin Roll dough (Chapter 1), refrigerated overnight

1 1/2 (5.5-ounce) cans tomato paste

1 1/2 tablespoons Dijon mustard

1 1/2 tablespoons gently packed light brown sugar

1 teaspoon sea salt

1 teaspoon ground black pepper

1 1/2 cups shaved ham, chopped into 1 1/2" pieces

1 3/4 cups grated sharp Cheddar cheese, divided

1/4 cup 2% milk

1. Remove dough from refrigerator and let sit at room temperature 15 minutes.

2. Dust flat surface with flour. Roll out dough into a 9" × 19" rectangle.

3. Spread tomato paste evenly over dough. Use back of a spoon to evenly spread Dijon mustard on top, then sprinkle with brown sugar, salt, and pepper. Evenly distribute ham and 1 1/2 cups Cheddar over dough.

4. Roll dough from long side into a tight tube. Slice into fifteen 1 1/4"-thick pieces using a bread knife.

5. Line a 14" roasting pan with parchment paper. Arrange slices in pan, cut side up, leaving 1/2" space between each. Cover pan with a tea towel and let sit 30 minutes.

6. Preheat oven to 375°F.

7. Brush roll slices with milk and sprinkle with remaining 1/4 cup Cheddar. Bake on lower rack 20 minutes until golden brown, then let cool 10 minutes before serving. Refrigerate leftovers in an airtight container up to 2 days.

Scrolls on Standby

These cheese scrolls can be stored in the freezer if you don't plan to gobble them up within two days. Place the scrolls into freezer-safe bags and store them for up to 2 months in the freezer. When you're ready to enjoy them, defrost in the microwave 2 minutes at 50 percent power.

Santa's Ledger Log

The Naughty or Nice List is filled to the brim with the dreams and wishes of everyone. And when you roll up this potato roulade, generously stuffed with a hearty Italian-flavored meat sauce, you best believe it will help you stay in everyone's good books! Here's a shortcut for busy elves: Swap in Italian sausages, cutting out the dried herbs and beef. Just chop, mash, and mix, and you'll trim down the effort without skimping on flavor and make a believer out of anyone.

SERVES 4

FOR POTATO ROLL

2 pounds russet potatoes, peeled and roughly chopped

1/3 cup unsalted butter, room temperature

2 large eggs, room temperature, divided

1/3 cup grated Parmesan cheese

1/2 cup 2% milk

1/2 cup sour cream

1 teaspoon sea salt

1/2 teaspoon ground black pepper

1/2 cup self-rising flour

1/2 cup cornstarch

1/2 teaspoon cream of tartar

1/4 cup confectioners' sugar

1. **To make Potato Roll:** Preheat oven to 350°F. Grease a 9" × 13" baking sheet with vegetable oil and line with parchment paper.

2. Place potatoes in a large saucepan over medium heat and cover with water. Cook 15 minutes until fork tender. Drain, then mash with butter in pan until smooth.

3. Separate egg whites and set aside. Stir egg yolks, Parmesan, milk, sour cream, salt, and pepper into potato mixture. Fold in flour and cornstarch until smooth.

4. In the bowl of a stand mixer, beat egg whites with cream of tartar on high speed, 1 minute, until stiff peaks form. Sift in confectioners' sugar and continue whisking 2 minutes. Gently fold into potato mixture with spatula.

5. Spread potato mixture on prepared baking sheet and bake 35 minutes. Remove from oven, cover with a damp tea towel, and set aside as you prepare filling.

continued

continued

FOR FILLING

2 tablespoons vegetable oil

1 large yellow onion, peeled and finely chopped

2 tablespoons freshly minced garlic

2 tablespoons red wine vinegar

1 pound lean ground beef

1 tablespoon smoked paprika

1 teaspoon crushed fennel seeds

$1/2$ teaspoon red pepper flakes

$1/4$ teaspoon dried thyme

$1/4$ teaspoon dried rosemary

$1/4$ teaspoon dried oregano

$1/4$ teaspoon dried ground sage

1 teaspoon sea salt

$1/2$ teaspoon ground black pepper

$3/4$ cup tomato sauce

2 cups shredded Cheddar cheese

$1/4$ cup grated Parmesan cheese

FOR GARNISH

$1/3$ cup sour cream

$1/4$ cup chopped fresh parsley

1 cup sauerkraut

6. **To make Filling:** In a medium pan over medium heat, heat oil and cook onion 10 minutes. Stir in garlic.

7. Pour in vinegar and use a wooden spoon to scrape bottom of pan to loosen any onion stuck to pan. Pour in 1 tablespoon water and stir to combine.

8. Push onions to the side of pan and add ground beef. Leave meat to brown 3 minutes, then reduce heat to low-medium.

9. Stir in smoked paprika, fennel seeds, red pepper flakes, thyme, rosemary, oregano, sage, salt, pepper, and tomato sauce. Cover and cook 5 minutes, then remove from heat.

10. With damp tea towel still in place, place a large cutting board on top of potato roll. Invert to release roll onto towel and remove parchment paper.

11. Layer potato roll with Cheddar and Parmesan, then beef mixture, leaving 1" around edges.

12. Using the tea towel as a guide, roll potato gently into a log from short end. Gently ease tea towel from under log.

13. **To Garnish:** Dollop sour cream and parsley on top. Serve hot with sauerkraut on the side.

14. Leftovers can be cooled 30 minutes then stored in an airtight container in refrigerator up to 3 days.

Energy Crisis Tuna Slices

When Christmas spirit is in crisis, Santa's elves must tinker up some sleigh-saving solutions. But when energy is crashing, just remember, it's what's inside that counts! And nestled inside many kitchen cupboards you'll find a trusty can of tuna ready to dash to your rescue in the nick of time. If you don't have a bottle of fish sauce, swap it out for soy sauce or Worcestershire sauce, and you'll be back on course in no time.

SERVES 4

2 garlic cloves, minced
$\frac{1}{2}$" knob fresh ginger, grated
1 cup chopped yellow onion
2 tablespoons fish sauce
1 large lime, zested and juiced
$\frac{1}{2}$ teaspoon ground chili
$\frac{1}{2}$ teaspoon sea salt
1 teaspoon granulated sugar
1 (15-ounce) can tuna in spring
    water
2 large eggs
$\frac{1}{2}$ cup panko bread crumbs,
    toasted
$\frac{1}{4}$ cup 2% milk

1. Preheat oven to 350°F.
2. In a large bowl, combine garlic, ginger, onion, fish sauce, lime zest and juice, ground chili, salt, and sugar.
3. Drain tuna and add tuna pieces to bowl. Break tuna apart with a fork and mix thoroughly.
4. In a small bowl, beat eggs, then add to tuna along with bread crumbs and milk. Stir the mixture together until well combined.
5. Line a 9" × 5" loaf pan with parchment paper. Scoop tuna mixture into pan and gently press surface to create an even layer.
6. Bake 35 minutes until the top is golden brown. Let rest in pan 10 minutes before slicing and serving.

Boardroom Tussle Tac-Ohs

Buddy is ready to welcome everyone with open arms, but following his faux pas in the conference room, an unexpected exchange was always going to be on the table! Having a spread with numerous taco fillings to cater to everyone's taste will keep you from being caught off guard. A spiced orange salsa brightly brimming with tangerine lends a surprising seasonal twist—it's nothing short of delicious. These small but oh-so-mighty taco bites can hold their own, so line up the shells and fillings and watch as everyone merrily charges back for more!

SERVES 4

FOR SPICED ORANGE SALSA
1 1/2 cups peeled and chopped
   tangerines
1 jalapeño, deseeded and finely
   chopped
1 teaspoon minced fresh garlic
1/3 cup finely chopped red onion
2 teaspoons honey
1/2 teaspoon ground ginger
1/4 teaspoon ground chili powder
2 tablespoons lime juice

FOR TACOS
1 tablespoon olive oil
1 large yellow onion, finely
   chopped
1 pound lean ground beef
1 (1-ounce) packet taco
   seasoning
1/4 cup water
12 mini taco shells, warmed
1 1/2 cups shredded lettuce
1/3 cup grated carrot
1/2 cup grated sharp Cheddar
   cheese

1. ***To make Spiced Orange Salsa:*** Place all ingredients in a food processor and pulse a few times until tangerines are chopped into finer pieces. Do not overprocess.

2. Salsa can be used immediately. However, for better flavor, transfer to an airtight container and refrigerate 2 hours, up to 5 days.

3. ***To make Tacos:*** Heat oil in a large frying pan over medium heat 3 minutes. Add onion and cook 3 minutes.

4. Add beef and cook 5 minutes, not stirring, then flip beef and cook a further 3 minutes.

5. Use a wooden spoon to break up meat. Sprinkle in taco seasoning before stirring in water. Cook 2 minutes until mixture thickens.

6. Layer taco shells with beef mixture, followed by lettuce, carrot, Salsa, and cheese, then serve. Alternatively, serve ingredients in bowls with shells on the side for people to fill as they choose.

Tickle Fight Tortellini

Serious moments are short-lived with Buddy around: He's always primed to pounce and transform any occasion into an opportunity for some mischief. With a sauce that's quickly turned around in just 10 minutes, this dish is set to tickle the taste buds and bring smiles to everyone around the table. To elevate store-bought tortellini, opt for hand-grated cheese rather than pre-shredded. Pre-shredded cheese is often coated with anti-clumping ingredients to maintain its form. You won't be laughing if your cheese sauce doesn't melt together!

SERVES 4

1 (18-ounce) package
   refrigerated cheese tortellini
1 tablespoon extra-virgin
   olive oil
1 cup chopped yellow onion
2 teaspoons chicken bouillon
   powder
1/2 cup chopped fresh parsley,
   divided
1 tablespoon lemon juice
1 teaspoon lemon zest
3 garlic cloves, minced
1 cup heavy cream
2 cups packed fresh baby spinach
3/4 cup freshly grated sharp
   Cheddar cheese
1/2 teaspoon sea salt
1 1/2 teaspoons ground black
   pepper
1/2 cup freshly grated
   Parmesan cheese

1. Cook tortellini according to package instructions. Drain and cover with lid to keep warm while making sauce.

2. Add oil to a large frying pan over medium heat and warm 2 minutes. Add onion and sauté 5 minutes.

3. Stir in chicken bouillon powder, 1/4 cup chopped parsley, lemon juice, lemon zest, and garlic. Cook and stir 2 minutes to allow liquid to evaporate.

4. Add heavy cream and stir 2 minutes. Add spinach and cook 2 minutes until wilted. Stir in grated Cheddar, salt, and pepper.

5. Divide tortellini onto four serving plates. Pour sauce over tortellini until well coated, then top with Parmesan and remaining 1/4 cup chopped parsley and serve.

CHAPTER 3

snacks and appetizers

There's room for everyone on the Nice List in your kitchen, especially when it's prepped with easy-to-serve snacks and appetizers! When the festive season brings a whirlwind of people through the door, unexpected surprises are always embraced, and everyone will feel welcome when you present the crowd-pleasers in this chapter.

When sweet cravings jump out like playful elves, you'll be ready with tempting bites like Little Buddy's Chex Mix or Hobbs Cob Loaf. If you are short on time, Son of a Nut-Crackle can be thrown together in the microwave in minutes. Meanwhile, Mr. Narwhal's Savory Tusk Twists—with their warm, doughy exterior and eye-catching blue filling—will rise up as a new festive favorite. And if guest numbers start to snowball, don't let the pressure mount: Both Snowball Rice Shots and Mailroom Mushroom Meatballs will hit the mark and are easy to assemble. Bring out a platter of assorted snacks and appetizers from the following pages, and you're sure to forge friendships wherever the season takes you.

Little Buddy's Chex Mix

Even Santa can find himself with an unexpected surprise. What to do when a guest pops in unanticipated?! You embrace the extra company with elf-like cheer! When friends or family become a delightful addition to your day, this popular party favorite of irresistible chocolate and peanut butter Chex mix will have everyone feeling welcome. Surprises are all part and parcel of the season, and in such merry moments, this simple treat not only satisfies cravings but also reminds everyone that sometimes the most spontaneous moments can be the most joyous.

SERVES 6

6 cups Corn Chex cereal
$1/4$ cup unsalted butter
1 cup dark chocolate chips
$1/3$ cup crunchy peanut butter
1 teaspoon vanilla extract
1 cup confectioners' sugar, divided
$1/2$ cup green and yellow M&M's

1. Pour Chex in a large bowl. Set aside.
2. In a small microwavable container, add butter and dark chocolate chips. Microwave 1 minute at 50 percent power.
3. Stir in peanut butter and microwave 1 minute at 50 percent power. Stir in vanilla.
4. Pour mixture over Chex and stir thoroughly to evenly coat. Sprinkle $1/2$ cup confectioners' sugar over Chex and stir to combine. Allow mixture to sit 30 minutes until chocolate is set.
5. Transfer to a serving bowl. Sprinkle remaining $1/2$ cup confectioners' sugar on top, followed by M&M's. Serve.

Son of a Nut-Crackle

A surprise snowball attack is no match for a trained elf. You can also be ready whenever sudden cravings hit, thanks to this sweet and salty treat. Microwavable crackle is a breeze, requiring just a quick raid of your cupboard for some basic ingredients. No special skills required! Just make sure to press the mixture as thinly as possible before it sets. If left too thick, larger chunks might be a hard surprise on your teeth!

SERVES 12

$1/2$ cup corn syrup
1 cup granulated sugar
1 tablespoon unsalted butter
1 teaspoon vanilla extract
2 cups Cocoa Krispies cereal
$1 1/2$ cups crushed roasted pecans
$1/4$ cup Christmas-colored
    nonpareils
$1 1/2$ teaspoons coarse sea salt

1. In a large microwave-safe bowl, stir together golden syrup and granulated sugar. Microwave 2 minutes on high. Stir, then microwave again $1 1/2$ minutes on high.

2. Stir in butter and vanilla and microwave $1 1/2$ minutes on high. Stir in Cocoa Krispies, pecans, and nonpareils and combine.

3. Scoop mixture onto a baking sheet lined with parchment paper. Place another sheet of parchment paper on top. Using oven mitts, press and smooth mixture as evenly and thinly as possible. Remove parchment paper, sprinkle sea salt evenly over surface and allow to cool at room temperature 1 hour.

4. Once cooled, break mixture into 1" pieces. Enjoy or store in an airtight container at room temperature up to 4 weeks.

Snowball Rice Shots

Buddy's time at the North Pole has armed him with a special skill, and bullies are no match for his snowball fighting talent. Even if this is your first time making this recipe, you'll hit your target on your first shot when you use plastic wrap to quickly twist the rice balls into the perfect shape. And if guest list numbers start to snowball, there's no need to freeze under pressure. This snack is easy to serve up, so you can toss together a double or triple batch.

MAKES 20 RICE BALLS

2 cups sushi rice
2 cups water
3 tablespoons vinegar
2 tablespoons castor sugar
$\frac{1}{2}$ teaspoon sea salt
$\frac{1}{2}$ cup soy sauce

1. Rinse and drain sushi rice in cold water 10 times until water runs clear and is no longer cloudy.

2. In a medium saucepan, combine rice and water and bring to a boil over medium heat. Once boiling, reduce heat to low-medium and simmer 15 minutes with lid ajar.

3. Turn off heat and let rice stand 5 minutes with lid on.

4. Mix in vinegar, castor sugar, and salt, and stir to combine. Set aside to cool 20 minutes.

5. Pour $\frac{1}{2}$ cup water into a small bowl to dip your fingers and spoon in as you shape rice into balls to keep rice from sticking. Fold a 12"-long sheet of plastic wrap in half.

6. Place plastic wrap in one hand and scoop 1 tablespoon rice into plastic wrap. Gather corners of plastic wrap together and twist to shape rice into a ball. Unwrap and set rice ball aside in an airtight container in the refrigerator until ready to serve, up to 3 hours. Repeat with remaining rice to make 20 rice balls.

7. Serve with soy sauce on the side for dipping.

A Fiery Shot

For a kick, serve up a feisty green wasabi mayonnaise for dipping instead of soy sauce. Stir together 3 tablespoons Kewpie mayonnaise, $1\frac{1}{4}$ teaspoons wasabi paste, 1 tablespoon mirin, $\frac{1}{8}$ teaspoon green food coloring, $\frac{1}{4}$ teaspoon Chinese 5 spice powder, and $\frac{1}{16}$ teaspoon salt. This sauce will keep in an airtight container in the refrigerator up to 1 month.

Magical Land Melts

Whether your guests have journeyed from as far as the frosty fields of the North Pole or from just around the corner, there's nothing quite like the comfort of a warm cheese dip to make anyone feel at home. To keep this dip invitingly gooey, serve it in a fondue warmer to maintain that melty magic. No fondue set? Nestle a larger heatproof glass bowl brimming with the cheese dip in a smaller bowl filled with two inches of hot (not boiling) water. Set this warm arrangement on a heat-resistant mat, keeping the comfort of a cozy dip within reach without any scalding surprises.

SERVES 4

2 tablespoons unsalted butter

1 teaspoon chicken bouillon powder

2 tablespoons all-purpose flour

1 cup 2% milk

4 ounces cream cheese block, roughly chopped

1 tablespoon lemon juice

2 tablespoons finely chopped fresh parsley

$1/4$ teaspoon sea salt

2 teaspoons mustard powder

2 (5-ounce) boxes Melba toast

1. In a small saucepan, melt butter over low heat. Stir in chicken bouillon powder and cook 30 seconds until well combined with butter. Add flour, whisking to form a smooth paste.

2. Gradually pour in milk, $1/4$ cup at a time. Continuously whisk 1 minute after each addition until mixture returns to a smooth paste.

3. Once milk is incorporated, add cream cheese. Stir 1 minute until cheese is melted into sauce, then turn off heat. Stir in lemon juice, parsley, salt, and mustard powder.

4. Transfer cheese dip to a serving bowl. Serve warm, accompanied with Melba toast.

Magical Munches

Add extra enchantment to your cheese dip with festively shaped tortilla crackers. Preheat oven to 375°F. Grab Christmas cookie cutters and press them into white tortilla wraps to create joyful figures. Lay the shapes on a parchment-lined sheet and brush both sides with olive oil. Bake 5 minutes, flipping once, until they're golden and crispy.

Mailroom Mushroom Meatballs

In a world that doesn't always sparkle like Santa's workshop, joy can be found in the most unexpected places—even a mailroom. When gathering your merry crowd, get the holiday snacks rolling by grating everything in advance. Packaged full of flavor, these bite-sized appetizers can be sorted into little bowls. Slide on a few skewers for easy handling. Once delivered to the family, they'll be given a jolly stamp of approval! To serve as a more substantial snack, divide the meatballs among serving bowls over white rice and top with finely sliced green onions.

MAKES 14 MEATBALLS

2 cups grated portobello mushrooms
¾ cup grated cabbage
½ cup finely chopped green onions
1 tablespoon freshly minced garlic
½ teaspoon ground black pepper
½ tablespoon ground ginger
½ teaspoon sea salt
1½ cups panko bread crumbs, toasted
1 tablespoon soy sauce
1 large egg

1. In a large bowl, stir together mushrooms, cabbage, green onions, and garlic. Sprinkle in black pepper, ginger, salt, and bread crumbs. Stir well before mixing in soy sauce and egg until combined.

2. Let mixture stand 15 minutes to allow bread crumbs to absorb moisture.

3. Use a tablespoon to scoop mixture, and use clean, damp hands to form into balls. Set aside on a large plate.

4. Heat 3 tablespoons oil in a large frying pan 3 minutes. Add meatballs to pan. Cook 7 minutes, using a spatula to turn over every 2 minutes until browned all over. Serve.

Mr. Narwhal's Savory Tusk Twists

A narwhal tusk towering among snowy glaciers is certainly a sight to behold, and these pastry twists will rise up to make an unforgettable appearance at your next Christmas gathering! Watch as they quickly capture the attention of your guests, filled with a blue ocean swirl of bean dip, and vanish just as magically as they appeared.

MAKES 12 TUSKS

2 tablespoons olive oil
2 teaspoons freshly minced garlic
2 teaspoons minced fresh rosemary
1 (15.5-ounce) can lima beans, rinsed and drained
¼ teaspoon ground white pepper
¼ teaspoon sea salt
¼ teaspoon blue food coloring
1 sheet (10") puff pastry

1. In a small frying pan over low heat, warm olive oil 1 minute, then add garlic and rosemary. Cook 1 minute.

2. Transfer to a medium bowl. Add beans and mash mixture together until a paste forms. Stir in white pepper, salt, and blue food coloring until evenly distributed throughout bean paste. Cover and refrigerate while you prepare puff pastry cones.

3. Preheat oven to 400°F.

4. Lay puff pastry on a clean surface and use a pizza cutter to cut pastry into 12 triangles, each with the widest base measuring 1½". Take each triangle and wrap around an oiled conical cream horn mold, starting with smallest point of triangle at the bottom and wrapping upward, slightly overlapping dough as you go.

5. Arrange wrapped pastry horns on a baking sheet lined with parchment paper. Bake 15 minutes until pastry is golden and puffed.

6. Remove sheet from oven and allow pastry horns to cool 10 minutes before removing from molds.

7. Fill a piping bag fitted with a large star-shaped tip with bean dip. Pipe dip into puff pastry horns. Serve.

Homemade Horns

If you don't have cream horn molds, create your own by shaping aluminum foil into cone-like structures and then wrapping each cone in parchment paper.

Hobbs Cob Loaf

Nothing is a match for the Hobbs family when they come together. Just like each family member plays a part in helping Santa, everything is put to work in this warm, sharable recipe. A simple round loaf of bread (known as a cob loaf in other countries) transforms into a bowl for the delicious dip. Its bready interior, once toasted, becomes the pieces for dipping! Meanwhile, the spinach dip, a reliable family gathering favorite, is given a twist to liven things up, just like the quirky relative at a festive feast.

SERVES 8

1 1/4 cups sour cream
1/2 cup mayonnaise
1 (8-ounce) package cream
    cheese, room temperature
3 tablespoons Dijon mustard
2 tablespoons lemon juice
1/2 tablespoon Worcestershire
    sauce
2 teaspoons freshly minced garlic
1/2 cup freshly grated Parmesan
    cheese
1 teaspoon sea salt
1 teaspoon ground black pepper
6 cups tightly packed fresh
    spinach
1 large bread boule (cob loaf)

1. In a large bowl, mix together sour cream, mayonnaise, cream cheese, Dijon mustard, lemon juice, Worcestershire sauce, minced garlic, Parmesan, salt, and black pepper.

2. Microwave spinach on high 30 seconds in a large microwave-safe bowl, then squeeze out excess liquid. Stir spinach into sour cream mixture.

3. Preheat oven to 350°F.

4. Cut top off bread boule and hollow out inside, leaving a thick shell. Place loaf and bread lid on a baking sheet. Tear interior bread into chunks and scatter them around bread bowl on baking sheet.

5. Spoon spinach mixture into hollowed-out bowl. Bake 25 minutes until bread is crispy and dip is heated through.

6. Transfer bread boule to a serving platter and surround with toasted bread pieces. Serve.

Ricotta Cotton Ball Bites

What those cotton balls tasted like remains a mystery, but Buddy's zest for zany treats is no secret! To bring out the big kid in everyone, roll these little bites—typically displayed as sophisticated bites of ricotta, roasted hazelnuts, and honey—in cotton candy. Feather light, they'll tempt everyone to mischievously sneak just one more. If you want to make them a bit more filling, serve them alongside a bowl of crostini. Guests can give their cotton balls a satisfying smoosh onto the little bites of toast for a bit more crunch.

MAKES 30 BALLS

1 cup ricotta cheese
1/4 cup crushed roasted
    hazelnuts, divided
2 teaspoons honey
2 ounces vanilla cotton candy

1. To drain ricotta, scoop onto center of a clean tea towel. Gather ends of towel and twist to close. Place in a small bowl and refrigerate overnight.

2. Remove ricotta from tea towel and transfer to a clean medium bowl. Add 3 tablespoons hazelnuts and honey and stir.

3. With wet hands, scoop a heaped 1/2 teaspoon of ricotta mixture and roll into a ball. Then roll in remaining hazelnuts to coat evenly. Place on a baking sheet lined with parchment paper. Repeat with remaining ricotta to make 30 balls. Refrigerate 1 hour to firm up.

4. Before serving, take a 12" × 4" strip of vanilla cotton candy and gently roll ricotta ball into center of candy. Place on a large serving plate. Repeat with remaining cotton candy and ricotta balls. Serve.

All the Trimmings Terrine

Lights and ornaments make any Christmas tree shine (including ones that have been not-so-legally taken from Central Park). This eye-catching terrine will light up with a sparkle reminiscent of a beautifully decorated tree when you include a bright layer of lemon juice gel to the middle. A flourish of lemon ribbon curls on top will remind guests of wrapped gifts nestled beneath the Christmas tree. If the time until your holiday celebration is ticking away quickly, just mix the lemon juice directly into the cream cheese mixture for a shortcut that still bursts with flavor—no need for the extra baubles of water, gelatin, and food coloring!

SERVES 10

1 (12-ounce) package smoked salmon
½ cup loosely packed fresh dill
½ cup finely chopped spring onions
½ cup finely chopped celery
1 teaspoon freshly minced garlic
1 (8-ounce) package cream cheese, room temperature
2 large lemons
¼ cup water
2 teaspoons gelatin powder
¼ teaspoon yellow food coloring

1. Line a 9" × 5" loaf pan with parchment paper. Layer salmon inside loaf pan, draping any remaining pieces over edges.

2. Rinse and dry dill, then roughly chop. Stems can be included but discard tougher stems at base.

3. Add dill to a medium bowl with spring onions, celery, garlic, and cream cheese. Use a fork to mix until well combined. Press half of cream cheese mixture into pan over salmon. Place in freezer 5 minutes to set slightly.

4. Use a lemon zest peeler to gently peel long ribbons of zest from around middle of each lemon, avoiding white pith. Curl zest ribbons around a straw and place in a glass of ice water to keep fresh and enhance curl.

5. Juice lemons to make ½ cup juice. Combine lemon juice with water in a microwave-safe measuring cup. Sprinkle gelatin powder on top and let sit 1 minute.

6. Microwave measuring cup on high 40 seconds, stirring halfway through. Stir in yellow food coloring.

7. Pour lemon gelatin mixture over cream cheese layer in loaf pan. Place back in freezer 10 minutes to set.

8. Spread remaining half of cream cheese mixture on top of set gelatin, smoothing with back of a spoon. Fold overhanging salmon edges over top of cream cheese. Place in freezer 10 minutes to firm.

9. Turn loaf pan onto a serving platter and garnish terrine with curled lemon zest ribbons. Serve.

"Code of the Elves" Christmas Crackers

While elves find singing the best way to spread Christmas cheer, others can agree that there are few better ways to spread joy than with a festive and tasty snack. With vibrant bursts of red sprinkled with snowy white sesame seeds, this "Code of the Elves" Christmas Crackers recipe will be a must for adding a touch of Christmas to any day of the year! Serve them up for a cheese platter guests will be unable to resist. If your cracker dough becomes a little too lively and springs back when rolled, it just needs a 5-minute rest before you're all set to roll the rest out with cheer.

MAKES 35 CRACKERS

1 cup all-purpose flour
1 teaspoon sea salt, divided
$1/3$ cup water
1 teaspoon red liquid food
   coloring
$1/4$ cup vegetable oil, divided
1 tablespoon sesame seeds
1 teaspoon ground sage
$1/2$ teaspoon onion powder

1. Preheat oven to 350°F. Line a baking sheet with parchment paper.

2. In the bowl of a stand mixer, stir together flour and $1/2$ teaspoon salt.

3. In a measuring cup, add water and stir in food coloring.

4. Stir food coloring into flour mixture along with 2 tablespoons vegetable oil for 1 minute until dough forms into a ball.

5. Dust flat surface with some flour and turn dough out onto surface. Use a rolling pin to roll dough to 6" × 18". Use a pizza cutter to cut dough into thirty-five 1$1/2$" × 2" pieces.

6. Transfer to prepared baking sheet.

7. In a small bowl, mix together sesame seeds, sage, and onion powder. Use a silicone brush to brush remaining 2 tablespoons vegetable oil onto each cracker. Sprinkle remaining $1/2$ teaspoon sea salt and sesame seed mix over crackers.

8. Bake on lowest rack 25 minutes. Turn off heat, open oven door, and leave crackers to cool 20 minutes before serving.

9. Crackers can be stored in an airtight container at room temperature up to 1 week.

Rising Steps and Stretch Bread

Buddy's eyes widen at the sight of continuously moving stairs—they can be a scary sight for anyone at first! If you're stepping into hosting for the first time and feeling a tad tentative, don't worry: This cheesy garlic pull-apart bread is so wide-eyed good that everyone will be eagerly stretching for more. The magic that elevates this bread to another level? Roasted garlic, a mellower and smoother flavor compared to the raw garlic typically found in cheese breads. If you know you'll be pressed for time on the day, roast the garlic up to four days in advance and store it in an airtight container in the refrigerator. Any unused cloves can be preserved in olive oil in a jar in the refrigerator for up to two weeks, ready to provide an uplifting experience to any savory dish they join.

SERVES 6

FOR ROASTED GARLIC
1 large head garlic
3 tablespoons extra-virgin olive
 oil

FOR PULL-APART BREAD
1/2 cup unsalted butter, room
 temperature
2 tablespoons Roasted Garlic
3/4 teaspoon sea salt
1 (9") sourdough loaf
14 ounces mozzarella cheese,
 cut into 1/4"-thin strips

1. **To make Roasted Garlic:** Preheat oven to 400°F.

2. Peel away outer layers of garlic bulb skin, leaving skins of the individual cloves intact, keeping bulb whole. With a sharp knife, slice 1/4" from top of bulb to expose individual cloves of garlic.

3. Place garlic bulb, cut side up, into a small ovenproof ramekin. Drizzle olive oil over garlic bulb, allowing oil to filter down between cloves. Cover ramekin with aluminum foil. Bake 30 minutes.

4. Remove aluminum foil and return garlic to oven to roast a further 15 minutes.

5. Let cool 15 minutes in ramekin before removing roasted garlic cloves from their skins.

6. **To make Pull-Apart Bread:** Preheat oven to 350°F. Line a medium baking sheet with parchment paper.

7. In a medium bowl, combine butter, Roasted Garlic, and salt until well mixed.

8. Make diagonal cuts into sourdough loaf every 1", cutting only halfway down through bread. Spread garlic butter mixture onto each piece of bread. Tuck a piece of cheese between each bread slice, reserving 8 pieces cheese.

9. Cut the loaf diagonally in the opposite direction to create diamond-shaped cuts in bread. Gently pull apart cuts and insert remaining cheese into new spaces.

10. Place loaf on prepared baking sheet. Cover bread with another sheet of parchment paper, then wrap sheet with aluminum foil.

11. Bake 25 minutes, then let cool 5 minutes before serving.

Smooth Serving

If the timing this season is going to be a bit of a stretch, plan ahead by making and freezing several loaves of this recipe. Wrap each loaf tightly in aluminum foil before freezing up to 3 months. When you're ready to serve, bake the frozen loaf, while still wrapped in foil, at 350°F for 35 minutes.

CHAPTER 4

dinner

You don't need to be raised by elves to know that there is a place for everyone at the dinner table! When chilly days are spent sledding and rolling up snowmen, the comfort of the recipes in this chapter promise a warm welcome home for everyone.

Glide through the holiday whirlwind with Kringle 3000 Chorizo Kebabs—a dish that keeps your energy bright and holiday spirits flying high. Then keep rolling through the season with Christmas-Gram Cannelloni and Papa Elf Pot Pies to deliver messages of seasonal joy straight to your family's taste buds. As you double-check that dinner list, with a thoughtful eye for everyone's tastes, you'll discover scrumptious recipes for all, from those ready to dive into Pulling Fried Dough Doubles to the vegetarian Nice List Nut Loaf. And don't let the "Impostor" Beef and Cheese Burgers fool you; their deliciousness will draw everyone together. After all, dinner isn't just about what's on the plate; it's about gathering the people you love together to share moments, laughter, and stories. Dig in as you recall fond memories of holidays past.

Papa Elf Pot Pies

Though Buddy heads off for grand adventures beyond the North Pole, Papa Elf is always there for a visit home. When you make them ahead of time, these hearty pot pies are patiently waiting for everyone after a day of zooming down slopes and frolicking in the snow! Gently tuck the sheet under a snug blanket of foil when baking to keep the crust from overbrowning. Feel free to substitute wine for a quarter cup of white wine vinegar.

SERVES 4

3 tablespoons olive oil, divided
1 pound bone-in, skin-on chicken thighs
1 teaspoon sea salt
1 1/4 cups diced carrots
3/4 cup diced celery
1 1/2 cups diced yellow onion
1 tablespoon minced garlic
1/2 cup dry white wine
1 cup chicken stock
1/2 cup heavy cream
1 tablespoon Worcestershire sauce
1/2 teaspoon ground black pepper
3 tablespoons gently packed light brown sugar
2 teaspoons dried thyme
2 teaspoons all-purpose flour
2 (10") sheets puff pastry, defrosted and halved
1 large egg
1 teaspoon water

1. Preheat oven to 425°F.
2. In a large pan over medium-high heat, add 1 tablespoon olive oil.
3. Sprinkle chicken with salt and place in pan, skin side down. Brown 6 minutes. Flip chicken and cook a further 6 minutes.
4. Set chicken aside in a large heatproof bowl and cover with a large plate.
5. Add remaining 2 tablespoons olive oil, carrots, and celery to pan and cook 5 minutes. Add onions and garlic. Sauté a further 1 minute until softened.
6. Add carrot mixture to heatproof bowl with chicken and re-cover.
7. Pour wine into pan. Use a spatula to scrape bottom of pan. Add in chicken stock, heavy cream, Worcestershire sauce, black pepper, brown sugar, and thyme.
8. In a mixing cup, combine 2 teaspoons flour with 1/3 cup liquid from pot to create a slurry. Add slurry to pan, whisking to combine until mixture thickens.
9. Remove bones and skin from chicken thighs. Dice into 1/2" cubes and add vegetables and chicken back into pan. Cook 10 minutes.
10. Place four 6-ounce ramekins on a baking sheet and fill ramekins with chicken mixture. Cover each ramekin with 5" puff pastry sheet so edges drape over. Brush pastry with an egg beaten with 1 teaspoon water. Use knife to pierce a hole in top of pastry.
11. Bake 12 minutes or until the pastry is golden. Allow to cool 5 minutes before serving.

Duet Dumplings

Just as a merry melody can draw in elves for a joyful chorus, these delicious dumplings are sure to set your taste buds singing. When submerged in a warm bath of broth, the flavors blend in perfect harmony, and the warm aroma will welcome everyone in from frightful weather. Served alongside Spiced Cranberry Dip, this recipe hits all the season's right notes!

MAKES 36 DUMPLINGS

FOR DUMPLINGS

1 cup ground chicken
1 ^{1}/2 cups grated cabbage
^{1}/2 teaspoon ground chili powder
^{1}/4 teaspoon ground ginger
2 teaspoons freshly minced garlic
^{1}/4 teaspoon sea salt
^{1}/4 teaspoon ground black
  pepper
36 dumpling wrappers
4 cups chicken stock

FOR SPICED CRANBERRY DIP

^{1}/4 cup cranberry sauce
^{1}/4 teaspoon Chinese 5 spice
  powder
1 tablespoon gently packed
  light brown sugar
1 ^{1}/2 tablespoons lime juice

1. **To make Dumplings:** In a large bowl, combine chicken, cabbage, chili powder, ginger, garlic, salt, and black pepper.

2. Spoon 1 teaspoon mixture into center of each dumpling wrapper. Dampen your finger in a bowl of water and run along edges of each wrapper. Use your fingers to fold each wrapper into a half-moon shape, pinching edges closed. Repeat to make 35 more dumplings. Set dumplings aside on a large plate.

3. Bring chicken stock to a simmer in a medium pot over high heat.

4. Slide a few dumplings at a time into simmering pot to prevent overcrowding. Let dumplings cook 3 minutes until they float to the top. Use slotted spoon to scoop out the cooked dumplings and place on plate. Repeat with remaining dumplings.

5. **To make Spiced Cranberry Dip:** In a small microwave-safe bowl, combine cranberry sauce, Chinese 5 spice powder, brown sugar, and lime juice. Microwave 30 seconds on high and stir. Serve alongside dumplings.

Emily's Family Chicken Dinner

Emily knows the secret ingredient to a memorable dinner isn't found in bustling holiday markets or on glistening store shelves but in who you enjoy it with! A simple chicken dinner can fill the home with mouthwatering aromas to help you draw everyone to the table. And in the midst of the holiday rush, even when everyone's got a bunch of stuff on their plate, it's important to pause and gather with family to savor the little moments together. Share in the dinner preparation, and then sit down to watch the magic of laughter and stories transform this recipe into something extraordinary.

SERVES 4

1/4 cup olive oil, divided
1 large yellow onion, peeled, halved, and sliced into 1/4" strips
1 tablespoon minced garlic
3 (6-ounce) boneless, skinless chicken breasts, cut into 1" cubes
2 tablespoons lemon juice
1/2 teaspoon sea salt
1 teaspoon ground black pepper
1 tablespoon finely chopped fresh rosemary
1 cup chicken broth, divided
2 large carrots, sliced into 1/4" coins
1 cup black olives, drained
4 white dinner rolls

1. In a heavy-bottomed pot over medium heat, heat 3 tablespoons olive oil 1 minute. Add onion and garlic and sauté 10 minutes until softened.

2. Push onion and garlic to one side of pan and add remaining olive oil to other side. Add chicken and brown 2 minutes, stirring to cook all sides.

3. Stir in lemon juice, salt, black pepper, and rosemary. Pour 1/2 cup chicken broth into pan. Use a wooden spoon to scrape bottom of pan 30 seconds.

4. Pour in remaining 1/2 cup chicken broth and carrots. Cook 5 minutes. Add black olives and warm 1 minute.

5. Remove from heat and serve alongside bread rolls.

Scene Stealer

If you're keen to stay true to the movie, asparagus makes another lovely side to this recipe. In a separate medium frying pan, add 1 tablespoon olive oil and 1 teaspoon minced garlic and cook 1 minute. Add in 1 pound asparagus and pour 1 tablespoon lemon juice over. Sprinkle with 1/2 teaspoon sea salt and 1/2 teaspoon ground black pepper. Cook 10 minutes, stirring every few minutes.

Pulling Fried Dough Doubles

As the big day draws near, Christmas activities ramp up both at the North Pole and at home. It's definitely no time to be short of helping hands! Everything hiding in your cupboard will be included in the festive flurry when you whip up a batch of these mini fried doughs. Watch as that overlooked can of chickpeas showcases its special talents, transforming into a star of your holiday spread. Make great use of all the spices lingering in the back of the pantry. And turn flour and a handful of other staples into a trusty dough that pulls more than its weight to keep stomachs satisfied.

MAKES 16 FRIED DOUGHS

FOR DOUGH
1 cup warm water, divided
1 teaspoon granulated sugar
1 teaspoon active dry yeast
2 cups all-purpose flour
1/2 teaspoon sea salt
1 cup vegetable oil

FOR FILLING
1 (16-ounce) can chickpeas, drained and rinsed
1/3 cup maple syrup
4 teaspoons gently packed light brown sugar
1 teaspoon ground cinnamon
1/2 teaspoon sea salt
1 teaspoon ground black pepper
1/8 teaspoon ground nutmeg
1/16 teaspoon ground cloves
1/2 teaspoon ground ginger
1 cup water, divided
3 garlic cloves, minced
1 cup thinly chopped yellow onion
1/4 cup fresh lime juice

1. **To make Dough:** In a measuring cup, stir together 1/2 cup warm water, sugar, and yeast. Set aside 10 minutes.

2. In the bowl of a stand mixer with a flat paddle attachment, combine flour, salt, and remaining 1/2 cup warm water. Add yeast mixture and combine, then change to a bread hook and knead 5 minutes until smooth and elastic.

3. Cover bowl with a damp tea towel and set aside 1 hour until doubled in size.

4. **To make Filling:** Add chickpeas to a medium saucepan over high heat. Stir in maple syrup, brown sugar, cinnamon, salt, black pepper, nutmeg, cloves, ginger, and 1/2 cup water. Cook 5 minutes. Add in garlic and onion, then cook a further 5 minutes.

5. Add remaining 1/2 cup water. Cover and simmer on low heat 15 minutes. Remove lid and simmer another 10 minutes until liquid has reduced.

6. Remove from heat and stir in lime juice. Cover with lid and set aside.

7. Punch down dough, divide into 16 golf ball–sized balls and flatten into circles.

8. Heat vegetable oil in a large frying pan, 3 minutes. Add a few dough circles at a time, cooking 1 minute until lightly brown, then flip to complete cooking 1 more minute on other side.

9. To serve, transfer Filling to a large bowl alongside a large serving plate piled with Dough.

Nice List Nut Loaf

Raised to welcome everyone wholeheartedly, Buddy knows there's always room for everyone on the Nice List. As you prepare for a merry gathering, remember to check your own list twice, paying special attention to those with dietary preferences! While the turkey might traditionally be the star of dinner, this year, make sure your vegetarian friends find a place at the table with a scrumptious nut loaf. Infused with festive flavors, this recipe is a warm welcome to many!

SERVES 4

1 cup walnuts, roughly chopped
1 cup whole almonds
2 (15-ounce) cans lima beans, including liquid
1/4 cup unsalted butter
2 cups chopped yellow onion
2 tablespoons minced garlic
5 teaspoons poultry seasoning
1 cup roughly chopped cranberries
2 large eggs, beaten
1/4 cup chopped fresh parsley
1/4 teaspoon sea salt
1/2 teaspoon ground black pepper
1 (14-ounce) can cranberry sauce

1. Preheat oven to 350°F.
2. Spread chopped walnuts and almonds on a large, unlined baking sheet. Roast 15 minutes, stirring halfway through.
3. Remove from oven and set aside to cool, 15 minutes.
4. Pour beans into a blender. Blend until smooth, then transfer to a medium bowl.
5. In a medium frying pan over medium heat, melt butter. Reduce heat to low and stir in onion, garlic, and poultry seasoning. Cook 5 minutes, stirring occasionally.
6. Add cranberries to onion mixture. Continue to stir and cook 5 minutes.
7. Remove pan from heat and combine roasted nuts, cranberry-onion mixture, and eggs into bowl with bean paste. Add parsley, salt, and black pepper, and mix well.
8. Spoon mixture into a loaf pan lined with parchment paper. Bake 45 minutes until loaf is firm and slightly browned on top.
9. Before serving, turn out cranberry sauce and spread to cover top of loaf. Slice and serve.

Ray's "Original" 11th Street Pizza

Santa hands out advice as generously as he does presents. The one golden nugget that sticks out when you're crafting the perfect night at home? Pizza. New York–style is meant to be foldable, so spread the sauce and toppings lightly and merrily, slice your pizza into four pieces instead of the usual eight, fold, and dig in!

SERVES 8

FOR PIZZA DOUGH
3 cups bread flour
1 tablespoon granulated sugar
1 teaspoon active dry yeast
1 teaspoon sea salt
1 cup warm water
$\frac{1}{2}$ cup extra-virgin olive oil, divided

FOR PIZZA SAUCE
3 tablespoons olive oil
1 teaspoon garlic powder
$1\frac{1}{2}$ teaspoons onion powder
1 teaspoon ground black pepper
1 tablespoon dried thyme
1 tablespoon balsamic vinegar
1 (4.5-ounce) can tomato paste
$\frac{1}{2}$ teaspoon granulated sugar
$\frac{1}{4}$ teaspoon sea salt

FOR ASSEMBLY
2 cups grated mozzarella cheese
2 cups grated provolone cheese

1. **To make Pizza Dough:** In the bowl of a stand mixer fitted with flat beater attachment, combine bread flour, sugar, yeast, and salt. Make a well in center of flour mixture and stir in warm water and $\frac{1}{4}$ cup olive oil.

2. Switching to dough hook attachment, knead dough 5 minutes.

3. Remove dough from mixing bowl and shape into a ball. Lightly oil bottom of bowl, then place dough back in bowl and cover with plastic wrap. Allow dough to rest 15 minutes.

4. Remove plastic wrap and knead a further 5 minutes. Reshape into a ball, re-cover with plastic wrap, and refrigerate overnight.

5. **To make Pizza Sauce:** In a small saucepan, heat olive oil over medium heat. Add garlic powder, onion powder, black pepper, and thyme. Stir until well combined and let mixture warm 1 minute.

6. Stir in balsamic vinegar, tomato paste, sugar, and salt, then remove saucepan from heat and let sauce cool 10 minutes.

7. Transfer cooled sauce to a sealable container and refrigerate overnight.

8. **To Assemble:** Remove dough and sauce from refrigerator 1 hour before making pizzas to bring to room temperature.

9. Preheat oven to 475°F. Place two pizza sheets inside oven to preheat.

continued

continued

10. Dust flat surface and hands with flour and split dough into 2 balls. Place 1 ball back into bowl and leave 1 on surface.

11. Use your hands to press down in center of dough and spread your fingers out to gently stretch dough outward. Work your way around dough, stretching it outward. Rotate dough a quarter turn and repeat stretching process. Continue rotating and stretching until pizza crust measures 12" in diameter. If the dough tears, use your fingers to gently press edges of tear together to form a seam. Repeat with second ball of dough.

12. Roll out 2 sheets of parchment paper and heavily dust with flour to keep pizza from sticking to paper. Place 1 crust on each piece of paper and spoon on pizza sauce, spreading it evenly with back of a spoon. Sprinkle both cheeses evenly on top.

13. Carefully remove one heated baking sheet from oven and place it on a trivet or tea towel to protect surface. Slide 1 pizza off parchment paper onto hot sheet. Brush pizza edges with 2 tablespoons olive oil and place it in oven. Repeat with second pizza.

14. Bake 10 minutes, rotating pizzas halfway through until cheese is golden and bubbling across the entire surface.

15. Remove pizzas and brush edges with remaining 2 tablespoons olive oil. Slice each pizza into 4 quarters and serve.

Secret Code Chicken Casserole

Clueless about matters of the heart? Luckily, Michael has a "secret code" that can help: Dates are about eating real food, far from the realms of candy canes and gumdrops elves are used to. But there's no reason not to swirl some sweetness into this dish! There is instant chemistry between the apricots and chicken, but the key to this Secret Code Chicken Casserole is using jam for an even flavor in each bite. Add rice to the mix to attract and bind everything together, and you have a scrumptious dish to share with the ones you love.

SERVES 4

2 1/2 cups shredded cooked
    chicken
1 cup uncooked white rice
1 cup chopped yellow onion
1 tablespoon freshly minced
    garlic
1/2 cup toasted almonds, chopped
1/2 teaspoon ground cinnamon
1 1/2 teaspoons ground ginger
1 tablespoon lemon zest
1/4 cup lemon juice
1 tablespoon unsalted butter
1 tablespoon all-purpose flour
1/4 cup hot chicken broth
1 (13-ounce) jar apricot jam
1 1/2 cups grated Cheddar cheese

1. Preheat oven to 350°F. Grease an 8" × 8" baking dish with butter.

2. In a large bowl, combine chicken, rice, onion, garlic, almonds, cinnamon, ginger, lemon zest, and lemon juice. Set aside.

3. In a small pan over low heat, melt butter. Whisk in flour and gradually add chicken broth to make a roux. Stir in apricot jam until combined.

4. Stir roux into chicken mixture and transfer to prepared baking dish, spreading evenly. Sprinkle grated cheese evenly over casserole.

5. Cook casserole, uncovered, 45 minutes. Cool 10 minutes before serving.

Snow Angel Soup

From paper cutout snowflakes around the home to the chance of a snowball fight worthy of a seasoned elf, frosted flakes bring a flurry of fun during the holidays. Whip up a cozy blizzard in a pot of creamy chicken and rice soup for your own fun in the kitchen. For a texture as smooth as a fresh snowfall, strain the soup through a large sieve. Then sprinkle a dusting of sugary magic on top using snow angel stencils to resemble a light snowfall. You'll want to serve the sprinkle at the table, as it'll dissolve as quickly as true snowflakes!

SERVES 4

2 tablespoons unsalted butter
1 1/2 cups chopped yellow onions
1/2 cup chopped celery
3/4 cup uncooked medium grain white rice
2 cups chicken stock
1/2 teaspoon dried thyme
2 bay leaves
1/4 cup granulated sugar
1 cup heavy cream
2 cups 2% milk
4 teaspoons Worcestershire sauce
1/2 teaspoon sea salt
1/4 cup confectioners' sugar

1. In a medium saucepan over medium heat, melt butter. Add onions and celery and cook 5 minutes, stirring occasionally.

2. Rinse rice under water three times before adding to saucepan. Stir in chicken stock and thyme, then press bay leaves into rice. Let mixture cook 10 minutes.

3. Pour in sugar, heavy cream, milk, Worcestershire sauce, and salt. Stir and cook 10 minutes. Remove from heat and discard bay leaves.

4. Scoop mixture into a large sieve over a large bowl and press gently to extract liquid. (Rice can be served as a side if enjoying for dinner.)

5. Divide strained soup among four serving bowls. Use snow angel stencils to dust a small amount of sifted confectioners' sugar evenly on top of each serving.

Purée Perfection

Don't want anything to go to waste? Skip the straining and purée the soup right in the pot using a stick blender for a chunkier, equally delicious meal!

Breaking News Report Ramen

A surprise cameo on the news puts an end to Jovie's night in with a warm bowl of ramen. In contrast to this headline-worthy moment, this ramen recipe prefers a slow news day, gradually developing its flavors overnight in a savory scoop. You won't want to set it down! Cover it in the refrigerator after cooking, and it'll be primed for a feature story on your weeknight menu.

SERVES 4

1 (6-pound) whole chicken
1 tablespoon olive oil
3 large carrots, chopped into $1/2$"-thick rounds
$2^1/2$ cups chopped green onions, divided
6 garlic cloves, crushed
$1/4$ cup chopped fresh ginger
5 star anise
2 (3") cinnamon sticks
5 whole cloves
1 teaspoon whole black peppercorns
1 tablespoon fennel seeds
15 dried shiitake mushrooms
1 (3" × 6") piece kombu/kelp
8 cups water
$1/2$ cup soy sauce, divided
1 tablespoon mirin
4 (4.2-ounce) servings uncooked ramen noodles
2 teaspoons toasted sesame oil
4 large soft-boiled eggs, halved

1. Debone chicken, storing breast and leg quarters in refrigerator for other recipe(s). Retain skin, frame, and wings.

2. Set Instant Pot® to sauté/sear. Pour in oil and heat 3 minutes.

3. Place chicken frame, skin, and wings in Instant Pot®. Cook 30 minutes uncovered to brown chicken.

4. Add carrots and 2 cups green onions to Instant Pot®, stirring to move them to bottom of pot. Cook 10 minutes.

5. Add garlic, ginger, star anise, cinnamon, cloves, peppercorns, fennel seeds, and mushrooms. Break kombu into smaller pieces and add. Pour in reserved liquid from chicken. Cover with water and stir in $1/4$ cup soy sauce. Set Instant Pot® to slow cook on low (8 hours).

6. Once done, strain through a sieve into a large bowl. Gently press solids to remove excess liquid. Discard solids. Skim and discard any fat from top of broth. Stir in remaining $1/4$ cup soy sauce and mirin. Set aside.

7. Cook noodles according to package instructions and drain. Divide noodles into four serving bowls. Top with broth. Drizzle $1/2$ teaspoon sesame oil onto each bowl.

8. Use remaining $1/2$ cup green onions to evenly garnish each bowl. Top each with an egg half and serve.

9. Broth can be refrigerated up to 1 week. Cool for 30 minutes before pouring into heatproof and airtight container. When ready to serve, reheat broth in a saucepan over low heat for 5 minutes.

Christmas-Gram Cannelloni

Singing telegrams are not for everyone, especially when they include a surprise revelation. Fortunately, this mouthwatering cannelloni stuffed with creamy ricotta and spinach won't bring unexpected surprises—though it will gather everyone around for a bite!

SERVES 4

FOR FILLING

9 ounces frozen chopped
    spinach, defrosted
1 1/2 cups ricotta cheese
2 large eggs
2 teaspoons minced garlic cloves
1 1/2 cups grated extra-sharp
    Cheddar cheese
1/4 cup grated Parmesan cheese
1 (8-ounce) box cannelloni tubes

FOR TOMATO SAUCE

1/4 cup unsalted butter
2 teaspoons minced garlic cloves
1/4 cup all-purpose flour
2 cups 2% milk
1 (6-ounce) can tomato paste
1/2 cup grated Cheddar cheese
2 teaspoons onion powder
1/2 teaspoon sea salt
1 teaspoon ground black pepper

FOR WHITE SAUCE

1/4 cup unsalted butter
1/4 cup all-purpose flour
2 cups 2% milk
1/2 cup grated Cheddar cheese
1/2 teaspoon sea salt
1 teaspoon ground black pepper
1/3 cup grated Parmesan cheese
1/4 cup fresh basil leaves

1. **To make Filling:** Preheat oven to 400°F.

2. In a large bowl, combine spinach, ricotta, eggs, garlic, and cheeses.

3. Fill a sandwich bag with mixture, cut off 1/2" corner of bag, and pipe filling into cannelloni tubes. Set aside on a large plate.

4. **To make Tomato Sauce:** In a medium saucepan over medium heat, melt butter 1 minute. Add garlic and cook 1 minute.

5. Stir in flour to form a paste, then gradually add 1/2 cup milk, stirring continuously. Mix in tomato paste, add remaining 1 1/2 cups milk, and cook 2 minutes, stirring frequently.

6. Add cheese, onion powder, salt, and pepper, and stir until cheese melts. Remove from heat and spread evenly on bottom of an ungreased 9" × 13" baking dish.

7. Place filled cannelloni side by side in a single layer on top of tomato sauce in baking dish.

8. **To make White Sauce:** In a clean medium saucepan over medium heat, melt butter and stir in flour to form a paste. Gradually add 1/2 cup milk, stirring until thickened, then add remaining 1 1/2 cups milk. Cook 2 minutes, stirring frequently.

9. Mix in cheese, salt, and pepper, and stir until cheese melts. Remove from heat and pour over cannelloni. Smooth out White Sauce with back of a spoon. Sprinkle cannelloni with Parmesan.

10. Bake 35 minutes until cheese is golden brown and a fork inserts into pasta easily with little resistance (pasta still holds shape). Garnish with basil before serving.

Peeping Present Peppers

Santa is well aware that children and elves alike are unable to resist a peek at anything they think is a Christmas present. And while the temptation to peek in the oven to check on dinner can be as strong as that eager excitement on Christmas Eve, don't lift the lid on this recipe! It can slow down the cooking time of the bell peppers roasting. Allow a full 30 minutes for them to bask in the warmth of the oven, and they'll emerge perfectly roasted, ready to be unwrapped by hungry family members.

SERVES 4

3 tablespoons unsalted butter, divided
1 cup finely chopped celery
1 garlic clove, minced
2 beef stock bouillon cubes, divided
1 cup pearl couscous
1 1/4 cups water, divided
4 large red bell peppers, rinsed
1 cup chopped yellow onion
1/2 cup chopped fresh parsley leaves

1. Preheat oven to 350°F.

2. In a medium saucepan over low heat, melt 1 tablespoon butter. Add celery, stir to coat, and cook 2 minutes.

3. Stir in garlic and 1 bouillon cube. Stir another 2 minutes to break down bouillon cube. Add couscous, stirring to coat it evenly. Cook 2 minutes.

4. Add 1/2 cup water and continue to cook 5 minutes, stirring halfway through cook time.

5. Pour in remaining 3/4 cup water along with remaining bouillon cube. Cook an additional 5 minutes, stirring occasionally to help bouillon dissolve. Remove pan from heat.

6. Slice off tops of peppers and remove seeds inside. Stuff peppers evenly with couscous mixture. Place tops back on peppers and arrange in an ovenproof pot.

7. Scatter remaining 2 tablespoons butter in dollops on bottom of pot and sprinkle chopped onion around peppers. Cover pot with an ovenproof lid and cook in oven 30 minutes.

8. Transfer each pepper to a serving plate, sprinkle chopped parsley over peppers and serve alongside cooked onions.

What's Your Favorite Bell Pepper Color?

Bell peppers come in a variety of colors, and each has its own unique flavor. Green bell peppers have a slightly bitter and grassy taste, whereas red, yellow, and orange peppers are sweeter and more fruity.

Kringle 3000 Chorizo Kebabs

When the world's belief in magic falters, a little tinkering is needed to supercharge Santa's sleigh. Should your own plans fly off course, you can assemble a merry medley of vegetables, cheese, and meat to rev the evening back up. Marinating over time will help soak up flavors, fine-tuning your dinner for peak flavor performance. But you can also hit the gas and grill these kebabs right away if you're as eager as an elf on Christmas Eve! The chili and chorizo bring a crackling fire of spice, so serve alongside a snowy dollop of Greek yogurt for dipping to keep things cool.

SERVES 4

9 ounces chorizo, cut into $1/2$"-thick half-moons

2 cups chopped bell peppers, mixed colors, seeded and cut into 1" pieces

8 ounces Halloumi cheese, cut into 1" × $1/2$" cubes

1 tablespoon lemon juice

4 teaspoons minced fresh garlic

$1/2$ teaspoon chili powder

$3/4$ cup extra-virgin olive oil, divided

4 teaspoons honey

1 cup plain Greek yogurt

1. On 12 kebab skewers, alternate threading chorizo, bell pepper, and Halloumi. Repeat until each skewer has three sets of each.

2. Place kebabs in a medium roasting pan, lining them up side by side so all kebabs touch bottom of pan.

3. In a small bowl, mix together lemon juice, garlic, chili powder, and $1/2$ cup olive oil. Drizzle evenly over kebabs. Refrigerate 2 hours to allow the flavors to infuse.

4. Place a grill pan over high heat and pour in remaining $1/2$ cup olive oil. Warm oil 3 minutes, then reduce heat to medium-high and place kebabs on grill pan. Cook 2 minutes, then flip and cook an additional 2 minutes.

5. Place 3 kebabs each onto serving plates and drizzle each serving with 1 teaspoon honey. Serve with yogurt on the side for dipping.

"Impostor" Beef and Cheese Burgers

There's nothing phony about an elf's excitement at seeing Santa. But the festive air can sizzle with surprise if it turns out that someone's masquerading as the big man in red! Although these lentil burgers certainly aren't trying to impersonate anything, the mushroom sauce adds a meaty flavor that might surprise everyone when they take their first bite. Nestled on buns, these undercover vegetable delights need only a cloak of Swiss cheese, a layer of lettuce, and a cap of sour cream to complete their merry disguise. Serve next to a pile of crinkle-cut fries with ketchup for dipping.

SERVES 8

1 (15-ounce) can lentils, drained
6 ounces mushroom gravy
2 teaspoons mushroom powder
1 cup finely chopped yellow onion
1 teaspoon minced fresh garlic
2½ cups panko bread crumbs, toasted
2 large eggs
1 (6-ounce) can tomato paste
¼ cup chopped fresh parsley
8 burger buns
8 slices Swiss cheese
8 large leaves romaine lettuce, washed and torn in half
½ cup sour cream

1. In a medium bowl, use a fork to combine lentils, mushroom gravy, mushroom powder, onion, garlic, bread crumbs, eggs, tomato paste, and parsley. Refrigerate mixture 2 hours to allow flavors to infuse and mixture to firm.

2. Preheat oven to 375°F. Line a baking sheet with parchment paper.

3. Form lentil mixture into 8 patties, about ¾" thick and 3" wide. Place on lined baking sheet.

4. Bake 30 minutes, flipping halfway through for even cooking.

5. To assemble burgers, place 1 patty on bottom half of each bun. Add 1 slice Swiss, 1 piece romaine lettuce, and 1 tablespoon cream. Top with remaining bun half. Serve.

Tucked-In Turkey Turnovers

Buddy's just trying to settle in with his new human family, but one of his bedtime traditions is amiss! When your taste buds are calling out for comfort during the Christmas season, tuck into these puff pastries with traditional Christmas flavors securely folded within. Make sure the filling is nestled in as snug as a bug by leaving a half-inch space around the edge—you don't want any filling escaping from under the pastry sheets!

SERVES 4

3 tablespoons unsalted butter, divided
12 ounces ground turkey
1/2 cup finely chopped celery
1 1/4 cups minced yellow onion
1 tablespoon poultry seasoning
1 teaspoon sea salt
1/2 teaspoon ground black pepper
1 teaspoon vegetable stock
3 (10") sheets puff pastry, defrosted
3/4 cup cranberry sauce

1. Preheat oven to 350°F.

2. In a medium frying pan, melt 1 tablespoon butter over medium heat.

3. Add turkey and use a spatula to break into smaller pieces. Cook 2 minutes, then stir. Leave to cook a further 2 minutes.

4. Add celery to pan and cook 2 minutes. Add onion, poultry seasoning, salt, pepper, and vegetable stock, and cook a further 5 minutes.

5. Cut pastry sheets on a diagonal into 4 triangles. On one half of each triangle, lightly spread cranberry sauce, leaving 1/2" space around edges. Spoon 1 tablespoon turkey mixture onto cranberry sauce and fold each pastry over to form a smaller triangle. Press to seal edges.

6. Melt remaining 2 tablespoons butter in microwave 15 seconds at 50 percent power. Brush turnovers with melted butter and bake 20 minutes. Cool 5 minutes before serving.

desserts

This Christmas, prepare for your home to be sprinkled with extra sweetness! With the recipes in this chapter, you can turn your kitchen into a sugary wonderland, filled with the sights and smells of desserts of every kind.

Start by checking off your holiday bucket list with Whole-Roll Cookie Dough Ice Cream. (While you can choose to eat it as fast as you can, you may find yourself wanting to savor every spoonful of this creamy, nostalgic treat.) Is the Christmas cookie choice proving too hard? There's no need to choose just one when you can serve up slices of Milk and Cookies Crumble Cake. And when the season's baking draws to a close, don't let those delicious scraps go to waste: pack them into VCR-Crammed Cookies for a yummy replay of all the best flavors the holidays have to offer. If you aren't sure which recipe you want to make first, remember that the sweetest joys are often the simplest—like sharing a spoonful of Sugarplum Spread. Sharing Christmas cheer is easy when the recipe yields extra jars!

Hobbs Holiday Gingerbread House

It seems that an elf was at work while Emily was away, creating a beautiful gingerbread display! When your family comes home, they can have a surprise awaiting them too. Arm them with extra icing and plenty of candies, and this gingerbread house will become a sugary spectacle in no time. Feeling really inspired? Whip up a second batch of gingerbread dough to make a two-story house, like Buddy's!

MAKES 1 GINGERBREAD HOUSE

FOR GINGERBREAD HOUSE
1/2 cup unsalted butter
1/4 cup boiling water
1/2 cup gently packed light brown sugar
1 large egg, room temperature
1/2 cup molasses
3 cups all-purpose flour
1 teaspoon baking soda
1/2 teaspoon sea salt
1 teaspoon ground cinnamon
3 teaspoons ground ginger
1 teaspoon ground cloves
1 teaspoon ground black pepper

FOR ROYAL ICING
2 large egg whites, room temperature
1/2 teaspoon cream of tartar
3 cups confectioners' sugar

1. **To make Gingerbread House:** In a medium saucepan over medium heat, melt butter in boiling water. Remove from heat. Stir in brown sugar, egg, and molasses. Set aside.

2. In the bowl of a stand mixer, combine flour, baking soda, salt, cinnamon, ginger, cloves, and pepper. Add wet mixture into dry mixture and mix to form a dough. Refrigerate in parchment paper 2 hours.

3. Preheat oven to 350°F.

4. Roll dough out to 1/4" thickness and cut two 4.75" × 6.5" rectangles (for roof), two 5.5" × 4" rectangles (for sides), and two 6" × 7" rectangles (for front and back).

5. Measure 4.25" up from bottom edge of each side piece and make a mark. On the top edge of dough, measure 3" across and make a mark in center. Use a pizza cutter or sharp knife to cut a triangle shape from each side point to center mark on top edge.

6. Slide cookie shapes onto a baking sheet lined with parchment paper and bake 15 minutes until firm to the touch but not hard. Let cool 1 hour before assembling.

7. **To make Royal Icing:** Whisk egg whites in large clean bowl of a stand mixer until foamy, then sprinkle in cream of tartar and mix 30 seconds. Gradually add confectioners' sugar and continue mixing on high until icing becomes thick and holds its shape.

8. Scoop icing into a plastic sealable bag and cut a small hole in one corner to create a piping bag. Apply icing to the edges of each gingerbread piece as you assemble Gingerbread House, starting with a front and side piece. Hold pieces together for a few seconds to allow icing to set.

9. Set Gingerbread House aside 6 hours to let icing dry completely before decorating as desired.

Milk and Cookies Crumble Cake

Could parents magically munch through mountains of cookies left out on Christmas Eve? Surely that's a feat only Santa himself could accomplish! If you find yourself in a cookie conundrum, embrace Santa's multicookie talents and merrily merge Christmas cookie classics into one dessert.

SERVES 8

FOR VANILLA SPONGE CAKE
1 cup unsalted butter, room temperature
$1/2$ cup granulated sugar
2 large eggs, room temperature
$3/4$ cup cake flour
$1/4$ teaspoon baking powder
$1/4$ teaspoon sea salt

FOR SHORTBREAD FROSTING
$3/4$ cup milk powder
$1/2$ cup unsalted butter
$2^1/2$ cups confectioners' sugar
1 teaspoon vanilla extract

FOR GINGERBREAD COOKIE BUTTER
10 (2") round gingerbread cookies
$1/2$ cup sweetened condensed milk
2 tablespoons unsalted butter, softened

FOR ASSEMBLY
12 Biscoff cookies, crumbled

1. **To make Vanilla Sponge Cake:** Preheat oven to 350°F. Line two 6" round cake pans with parchment paper.

2. In a large bowl, cream together butter and granulated sugar 5 minutes until light in color. Add eggs and mix. Scrape sides of bowl.

3. In a separate medium bowl, sift together flour and baking powder. Stir in salt.

4. Gradually add dry mixture to wet mixture and stir until well combined. Divide batter equally between prepared pans.

5. Bake 25 minutes or until a skewer inserted in center comes out clean.

6. Allow cakes to cool in pans 10 minutes before transferring to a cooling rack to cool 30 minutes.

7. **To make Shortbread Frosting:** Preheat oven to 350°F.

8. Sprinkle milk powder evenly over a large, unlined baking sheet. Bake 10 minutes, then stir and bake 10 minutes until golden brown. Set aside to cool 10 minutes.

9. In a medium bowl, cream together butter and confectioners' sugar. Add toasted milk powder and vanilla. Mix until well combined, then set aside.

10. **To make Gingerbread Cookie Butter:** Add gingerbread cookies to a food processor and pulse into a coarse powder. Add butter and condensed milk and pulse until a smooth paste forms, about 1 minute.

11. **To Assemble:** Place one Cake on a large serving plate. Spread Gingerbread Cookie Butter on top. Spread $1/2$ Shortbread Frosting over Gingerbread Cookie Butter. Place second Cake on top. Coat top and sides with remaining Shortbread Frosting. Sprinkle crumbled Biscoff cookies on top. Serve or refrigerate up to 3 days.

Sugarplum Spread

Buddy twinkles with the knowledge that life's sweetest joys are often found in the simplest of moments—like sneaking a spoonful of your favorite spread straight from the jar. But it's better when you're sharing the moment with someone else. Fortunately, spreading little moments of Christmas cheer becomes a piece of cake when you sandwich this Sugarplum Spread between slabs of sponge cake or dollop it onto pieces of toast. This recipe makes two jars, so you can also share Christmas cheer beyond your family.

MAKES 2 CUPS

1 cup plum jam
1 cup sweetened condensed
    coconut milk
1 teaspoon ground cardamom
1/2 teaspoon ground ginger
2 tablespoons fresh lime juice
1/4 teaspoon rose pink food
    coloring
1/2 teaspoon lemon extract

1. In a medium saucepan over medium heat, combine plum jam, coconut milk, cardamom, and ginger. Cook 15 minutes, whisking until plum jam has dissolved.

2. Turn off heat and stir in lime juice, food coloring, and lemon extract. Let cool 15 minutes before pouring into two 8-ounce jars.

3. Cool jars in refrigerator 2 hours to set, store up to 2 weeks.

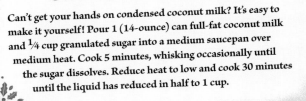

Condensed Concoction

Can't get your hands on condensed coconut milk? It's easy to make it yourself! Pour 1 (14-ounce) can full-fat coconut milk and 1/4 cup granulated sugar into a medium saucepan over medium heat. Cook 5 minutes, whisking occasionally until the sugar dissolves. Reduce heat to low and cook 30 minutes until the liquid has reduced in half to 1 cup.

Elf Culture Eggnog Éclairs

Have you found someone with a love of elf culture? Share in this affinity by enjoying a luscious Elf Culture Eggnog Éclair together! You might initially feel skeptical; surely magic is involved in piping delicate choux pastry at home? They're actually quite easy to make, so don't whisk away the idea. Bake up a batch and watch in delight as friends and family bond over these seasonally flavored éclairs. They'll be the shining star that will light up everyone's tummies!

MAKES 8 ÉCLAIRS

FOR EGGNOG CREAM
1¾ cups heavy cream, divided
4 large egg yolks
⅓ cup granulated sugar
1 teaspoon ground nutmeg, divided
¾ cup sifted confectioners' sugar
2 tablespoons brandy flavoring

FOR CHOUX PASTRY
½ cup water
½ cup 2% milk
½ cup unsalted butter
1 tablespoon granulated sugar
½ teaspoon sea salt
1 cup all-purpose flour
4 large eggs, room temperature

FOR GLAZE
1 cup confectioners' sugar
3 tablespoons 2% milk
1 teaspoon vanilla extract
5 teaspoons gold pearlized sugar sprinkles

1. **To make Eggnog Cream:** Heat 1 cup heavy cream in a small saucepan over low heat 3 minutes until warm.

2. Whisk together egg yolks, sugar, and ½ teaspoon nutmeg in a large measuring cup. Pour ¼ cup cream into egg yolk mixture, whisking to temper eggs.

3. Pour egg yolk mixture into saucepan with remaining ½ cup cream. Cook over low heat, constantly whisking, 10 minutes until mixture is steaming and begins to bubble but isn't boiling. If mixture begins to overheat, remove from heat and whisk in some cold cream to reduce heat.

4. Transfer to a large airtight container and refrigerate 3 hours.

5. Pour into a large bowl with confectioners' sugar, brandy flavoring, and remaining ½ teaspoon nutmeg. Whisk on high 3 minutes until cream forms firm peaks. Refrigerate in an airtight container until ready to use, up to 2 days.

6. **To make Choux Pastry:** Preheat oven to 375°F. Place a rimmed baking sheet on bottom rack and fill with 1" water. Line two baking sheets with silicone mats and set aside.

7. In a large saucepan over medium heat, mix together water, milk, butter, sugar, and salt. Cook 7 minutes until mixture comes to a boil.

8. Stir in flour quickly 1 minute until dough comes together to form a soft paste. It will pull away from saucepan and not stick to spoon when ready. Transfer to a large bowl of a stand mixer and let cool 5 minutes. Stir on low speed halfway through cooling to release heat.

continued

continued

9. On low speed, add one egg at a time to Pastry, mixing 1 minute before adding each egg.

10. Spoon Pastry into a large piping bag fitted with a large, star-shaped tip. Pipe out some Pastry onto lined baking sheets to measure 1 1/2" wide × 5" long. You'll get the extra 1/2"-wide Pastry by piping it out slowly so there is time for it to spread outward. Repeat to create 8 lines of Pastry.

11. Bake one sheet at a time 35 minutes on second-lowest oven rack. Remove from oven and cool 20 minutes.

12. Use a serrated knife to slice top of each éclair lengthwise. Spoon filling into éclair and close top. Set aside.

13. **To make Glaze:** In a measuring cup, combine confectioners' sugar, milk, and vanilla. Whisk until smooth, then pour into a low wide bowl.

14. Dip top of each Éclair into Glaze and sprinkle with sugar sprinkles. Refrigerate Éclairs 40 minutes until Glaze is dry to the touch. Serve.

Elf Magic Éclairs

If you find yourself dashing through the holiday rush but still looking to spread some tasty cheer, here's a shortcut. Whip up the Eggnog Cream and Glaze and use premade éclair pastry shells. It'll seem like you've conjured up some Christmas magic in the blink of an eye!

Whole-Roll Cookie Dough Ice Cream

In the whirlwind of the festive season, there isn't always time for everything on your to-do list. A little condensing becomes essential to savor every moment. Swirl cookie dough into a no-churn ice cream, and you and your loved ones can swiftly (and deliciously) check off your dessert cravings with a two-in-one treat.

SERVES 4

1 cup all-purpose flour
6 tablespoons unsalted butter, room temperature
6 tablespoons gently packed light brown sugar
1/4 cup granulated sugar
3 teaspoons vanilla extract, divided
1/2 teaspoon sea salt
1/4 cup milk chocolate chips
1 (14-ounce) can sweetened condensed milk
2 1/2 cups whipping cream

1. In a measuring cup, microwave flour 1 minute at 50 percent power, stirring halfway through.

2. In the bowl of a stand mixer, cream together butter, brown sugar, and granulated sugar. Mix in 1 teaspoon vanilla. Mix in salt and flour until blended. Stir in chocolate chips, then set aside.

3. In a clean medium bowl, whisk together condensed milk, remaining 2 teaspoons vanilla, and whipping cream 3 minutes until cream creates peaks that hold form. Fold in cookie dough.

4. Pour mixture into a 9" × 5" loaf pan lined with parchment paper. Freeze 2 hours before serving.

Christmas Cookie Bliss

This recipe makes the traditional chocolate chip cookie dough, but it's easy to adapt your favorite holiday cookie recipe! Quarter a two-dozen cookie recipe of your choice, microwave flour 1 minute at 50 percent power to heat-treat, and omit any eggs before continuing with step 4 of this recipe.

Shoemaker's Secret Plum Cobbler

It's a well-known fact that elves are excellent craftspeople who do their best work during the night in secret. So when the beginning of this cobbler appears in the refrigerator the next morning, your family might think elves have been at work! But every baker knows magic happens when everyone's asleep. This gives the spices time to infuse in the fruit, making the flavors even more spectacular. So stir together the fruit mixture before you go to bed, and you'll have a lovely plum cobbler ready to bake and enjoy the next day. Top each warm serving with a large scoop of vanilla ice cream.

SERVES 4

2 (15-ounce) cans whole plums, drained and pitted
2 tablespoons orange peel zest
3 teaspoons vanilla extract, divided
1/3 cup honey
2 teaspoons grated lime zest
2 tablespoons lime juice
2 teaspoons ground cinnamon
1/4 teaspoon ground cloves
1/2 teaspoon ground nutmeg
1/4 cup cornstarch
1 cup all-purpose flour
1 teaspoon baking powder
1/4 cup granulated sugar
1/4 teaspoon sea salt
3 tablespoons vegetable oil
1 large egg, beaten
1 cup 2% milk

1. Preheat oven to 375°F.

2. In a large mixing bowl, stir together plums, orange peel zest, 2 teaspoons vanilla, honey, lime zest, and lime juice. In a small bowl, stir together cinnamon, cloves, nutmeg and cornstarch to combine, before stirring through plum mixture.

3. Pour plum mixture into an 8" × 8" baking dish, spreading it evenly, and refrigerate overnight.

4. When ready to bake, in a separate large bowl, sift together flour and baking powder, then stir in sugar and salt.

5. Add vegetable oil, egg, milk, and remaining 1 teaspoon vanilla to dry ingredients. Stir until batter is smooth. Pour evenly over plum mixture in baking dish. Bake 40 minutes.

6. Remove from oven and let cool 5 minutes. Scoop into 4 small bowls and serve.

Spiced Raccoon Yule Roll

Not everyone is ready for an elf's level of enthusiasm. But the warm embrace of a traditional holiday dessert is sure to win over feisty spirits! Infused with gingerbread spices, this cake roll is sure to be a favorite among the ones you love. Keep a damp tea towel within arm's reach for the crucial moment when you turn out the sponge cake. Roll it back up swiftly, all snuggled up in the tea towel, to keep it from cracking as it cools.

SERVES 6

FOR SPONGE CAKE
3/4 cup sifted cake flour
1 1/2 teaspoons ground cinnamon
3 teaspoons ground ginger
1 teaspoon ground cloves
1 teaspoon ground black pepper
1 teaspoon baking powder
1/4 teaspoon sea salt
3 large eggs, yolks and whites
    separated
1 cup confectioners' sugar,
    divided
1 teaspoon vanilla extract
1/4 cup granulated sugar

FOR FROSTING
1 1/2 tablespoons instant coffee
1/4 cup boiling water
1 teaspoon vanilla extract
1 tablespoon unsalted butter,
    room temperature
4 cups plus 1 tablespoon
    confectioners' sugar, divided
1/4 cup cocoa powder
12 green and yellow gumdrops
1/4 cup mini marshmallows
1 tablespoon edible holly
    sprinkle mix

1. **To make Sponge Cake:** Preheat oven to 400°F. Line a 12" × 14" baking sheet with parchment paper.

2. Dampen a clean tea towel and lay out on a clean surface.

3. In a large bowl, sift together cake flour, cinnamon, ginger, cloves, black pepper, baking powder, and salt. Set aside.

4. In the bowl of a stand mixer, whisk egg whites 1 minute on medium-high speed until foamy. Sift in 1/2 cup confectioners' sugar and whisk 2 minutes until firm peaks form.

5. In a third large bowl, whisk egg yolks and vanilla 1 minute. Sift in remaining 1/2 cup confectioners' sugar and whisk 1 minute.

6. Fold half of dry ingredients into egg yolk mixture using a rubber spatula until all ingredients are gently folded together.

7. Gently fold in half of egg white foam. Repeat with remaining dry ingredients, then finish with remaining egg white foam.

8. Pour and smooth batter evenly onto prepared sheet. Bake 6 minutes until Cake is light golden in color and springs back when gently touched.

9. Sprinkle damp tea towel with granulated sugar.

10. Remove Cake from oven and turn out onto tea towel. Gently peel off parchment paper and roll up Cake in tea towel. Leave 25 minutes to cool before frosting.

11. **To make Frosting:** In a small mug, stir together instant coffee and boiling water. Set aside to cool, 15 minutes.

continued

continued

12. In a stand mixer bowl, beat together butter, vanilla, 4 cups confectioners' sugar, cocoa powder, and coffee until a smooth, fluffy cream forms.

13. Unroll cake, spread with ½ of frosting, and reroll without tea towel. Cut ends with bread knife to make even. Transfer to serving platter, then cover entire roll with thin layer of frosting to keep crumbs out of final layer of frosting.

14. Chill roll in refrigerator 20 minutes to set. Apply remaining frosting in a thick layer and use a fork to create bark-like texture through the frosting. Dust with remaining 1 tablespoon confectioners' sugar and top with mini marshmallows, gumdrops and sprinkle mix. Chill for a further 20 minutes to set before serving.

15. You can make this the night before, leaving decorations off and storing overnight in refrigerator covered with a damp tea towel. Just decorate before serving. Once sliced, store leftovers in refrigerator up to 3 days in an airtight container.

Oak Oven Oatmeal Cookies

It might be time for elves to find another gig—or, at the very least, another place to bake cookies. Baking in an oak tree during fire season would certainly backfire! These cookies won't set your house on fire, but their warm aroma is sure to have the family come running. Rekindle everyone's taste buds this Christmas season and fuel them up for opening presents with these toasty, chai-glazed oatmeal cookies studded with cranberry bits. A regular oatmeal cookie is certainly no match!

MAKES 24 COOKIES

FOR OATMEAL COOKIES
2 cups all-purpose flour
1 teaspoon baking soda
1 teaspoon baking powder
$\frac{1}{2}$ teaspoon sea salt
1 cup granulated sugar
1 cup gently packed light brown sugar
$\frac{1}{2}$ cup dried cranberries
2 cups old-fashioned rolled oats
2 large eggs, beaten, room temperature
1 teaspoon vanilla extract
1 cup unsalted butter, melted

FOR CHAI SPICE GLAZE
3 tablespoons 2% milk, warm
1 teaspoon gently packed light brown sugar
$\frac{1}{2}$ teaspoon red food coloring
1 teaspoon vanilla extract
1$\frac{1}{2}$ cups confectioners' sugar
2 teaspoons chai spice powder

1. **To make Oatmeal Cookies:** Preheat oven to 350°F.
2. In a large bowl of a stand mixer, sift together flour, baking soda, and baking powder. Add salt, granulated sugar, brown sugar, cranberries, and oats and mix. Add eggs and mix.
3. In a small bowl, stir vanilla into melted butter and add to flour mixture. Mix well.
4. Scoop dough into 24 (1") balls and place on 3 baking sheets lined with parchment paper, leaving 2" between each cookie ball. Do not press down on dough.
5. Bake 15 minutes until lightly golden and a toothpick inserted in center comes out clean. Allow cookies to cool 5 minutes on sheets before transferring to a cooling rack to cool a further 15 minutes.
6. **To make Chai Spice Glaze:** In a small bowl, stir together milk and brown sugar until sugar dissolves. Stir in red food coloring and vanilla.
7. In a separate medium bowl, sift confectioners' sugar and chai spice powder. Whisk in wet ingredients until smooth.
8. Use a teaspoon to drizzle Chai Glaze over cooled Cookies. Allow Glaze to dry 10 minutes. Let Cookies cool 2 hours before storing in an airtight container at room temperature up to 1 week.

Seasonally Spicy

Make your own chai spice powder by stirring together 1 tablespoon Chinese 5 spice powder, 1 teaspoon ground cardamom, $\frac{1}{4}$ teaspoon ground ginger, $\frac{1}{4}$ teaspoon ground nutmeg, 1$\frac{1}{2}$ teaspoons black tea leaves, and $\frac{1}{2}$ teaspoon ground cinnamon. Store in a small airtight container at room temperature up to 4 weeks.

VCR-Crammed Cookies

Fast-forward to the end of your Christmas baking marathon when you're left with a handful of nuts and a hodgepodge of festive bits and bobs. You toss all these ingredients together to create a cookie that captures the highlight reel of the season's most magical flavors! Guests will be cramming these tasty cookies straight into their mouths (and hopefully not the VCR)!

MAKES 24 COOKIES

2 cups all-purpose flour
$1/2$ teaspoon baking soda
$1/2$ teaspoon baking powder
$1/2$ teaspoon sea salt
$1/2$ teaspoon ground nutmeg
$1/4$ teaspoon ground cloves
1 teaspoon ground cinnamon
$1/2$ cup unsalted butter, softened
$1\frac{1}{2}$ cups gently packed light
    brown sugar
1 teaspoon vanilla extract
3 large eggs, room temperature
$1/4$ cup desiccated coconut
1 cup Rice Krispies
1 cup dried cranberries
$1/2$ cup candied citrus peel
$1/2$ cup green candied cherries
$1/2$ cup pecans, roughly chopped

1. Preheat oven to 350°F. Line 3 baking sheets with parchment paper.

2. In a large bowl, sift together flour, baking soda, baking powder, salt, nutmeg, cloves, and cinnamon.

3. In mixing bowl of a stand mixer, cream together butter, brown sugar, and vanilla until light and fluffy. Mix in eggs until combined.

4. Gradually mix in dry ingredients. Stir in coconut, then Rice Krispies. Stir in cranberries, citrus peel, cherries, and pecans.

5. Drop 24 spoonfuls of dough onto lined baking sheets, leaving 2" between dough. Use a fork to gently press down on each cookie. Bake 20 minutes until lightly browned.

6. Allow to cool on sheets 10 minutes before transferring to a wire rack to cool 2 hours. Serve or store in an airtight container at room temperature up to 3 days.

Christmas Checklist Cheesecake

As you glide from one festivity to the next, mirror the winter wonderland around you with an ice blue glaze on a classic cheesecake. Like Buddy's New York snow globe, each slice glistens, decked with sugar pearls, snowflakes, and snowy peaks of cream. For busy elves buzzing about, bypass glazing and instead whisk a half teaspoon of blue food coloring into the cream. Pipe blue bursts onto snow-white cheesecake, still capturing frosty fun in a fraction of the time.

SERVES 8

FOR ALMOND CRUST

1 1/2 cups almond flour
1/4 cup gently packed light brown sugar
1/4 teaspoon sea salt
1/4 cup unsalted butter, melted
1/2 teaspoon vanilla extract

FOR CHEESECAKE

4 (8-ounce) packages cream cheese, room temperature
1 cup granulated sugar
1 teaspoon vanilla extract
4 large eggs

FOR ASSEMBLY

2 teaspoons gelatin powder
1/2 cup water
1 cup castor sugar
3/4 cup heavy cream
3/4 cup white chocolate candy melts
1 teaspoon blue food coloring
1 batch Nougat Cream from Arctic Puffin Pancakes (Chapter 1)
2 tablespoons confectioners' sugar
1/2 teaspoon mini silver sugar pearls
1 teaspoon white snowflake sprinkles
1 teaspoon blue sugar pearls

1. **To make Almond Crust:** Preheat oven to 350°F.

2. Cut a circle of parchment paper slightly larger than the base of a 9" springform pan. Cut a long strip of parchment paper to line pan's sides. Lightly grease inside of unhinged pan with butter. Place parchment paper on base and around sides, then reassemble pan.

3. In a medium bowl, combine almond flour, brown sugar, and salt. Stir in melted butter and vanilla until well combined. Press firmly into bottom of prepared pan.

4. Bake crust 10 minutes, then let cool 1 hour.

5. **To make Cheesecake:** Preheat oven to 325°F.

6. In a large bowl, beat cream cheese with granulated sugar and vanilla until combined. Add eggs, one at a time, mixing on low speed until combined.

7. Pour mixture over cooled crust and bake 55 minutes. Cheesecake will be set around edges but will have a slight wobble in middle. Cool in pan 15 minutes to finish setting before removing pan sides. Refrigerate cheesecake on pan base 4 hours.

8. **To Assemble:** In a small bowl, sprinkle gelatin over water. Let sit 1 minute, then microwave 40 seconds, stirring halfway through cooking.

9. Transfer to a medium saucepan, then add castor sugar and stir over medium heat 2 minutes until dissolved. Stir in heavy cream and cook another 2 minutes.

10. Remove pan from heat, add white chocolate melts, and stir 1 minute until melted. Mix in blue food coloring until color is fully blended.

continued

continued

11. Let glaze cool to room temperature 25 minutes, stirring occasionally until thick yet pourable.

12. Slide Cheesecake from pan base onto a wire rack with a baking sheet underneath. Pour glaze over Cheesecake evenly. Refrigerate on wire rack and pan 15 minutes to set glaze.

13. Pipe Nougat Cream around outer rim of Cheesecake using a piping bag fitted with a star-shaped tip. Dust Cheesecake with confectioners' sugar and decorate with mini silver sugar pearls, snowflake sprinkles, and blue sugar pearls.

14. Transfer Cheesecake to a serving platter to slice and serve. Leftover Cheesecake can be stored in refrigerator up to 3 days.

Elves' Four Food Groups Fudge

An elf's sweetness has to come from somewhere—and it seems candy, candy canes, candy corns, and syrup are at the foundation! Sink your teeth into elf culture with a maple-flavored fudge generously topped with festive favorites. Candied to the max, this fudge might just bubble over with sweetness in the microwave, echoing the same enthusiasm you'd expect from an elf. Using a large bowl is key to give the mixture enough space to expand and collapse back down. And don't dance away from the microwave: Keep a watchful eye as it cooks. If it looks like it might overflow, just take it out, whisk, and then continue microwaving.

MAKES 18 PIECES

1 cup castor sugar
1/2 (14-ounce) can sweetened
    condensed milk
1/4 cup unsalted butter
1/2 teaspoon sea salt
1 teaspoon cake batter extract
1 teaspoon maple extract
1/2 cup white chocolate chips
1 tablespoon crushed candy
    canes
1 tablespoon candy corn
1 tablespoon red and green
    M&M's

1. Line a 9" × 5" loaf pan with parchment paper.
2. In a microwavable 4.5-quart glass bowl, mix together sugar, condensed milk, and butter. Microwave 7 minutes on high, stopping to whisk every minute.
3. Whisk in salt, cake batter extract, and maple extract, then pour into prepared loaf pan.
4. In a microwavable glass measuring cup, add white chocolate chips and microwave 1 minute at 50 percent power. Stir until completely melted, then pour over fudge mixture and smooth surface with a spatula. Sprinkle candy canes, candy corn, and M&M's over top.
5. Refrigerate 1 hour until set, then slice into eighteen 1 1/2" cubes. Store in an airtight container at room temperature up to 2 weeks.

Too Much of a Good Thing

You can make a second batch of this recipe to finish off the can of condensed milk, but don't try to double the batch in one bowl; otherwise, the fudge will overflow as it bubbles up!

Sugary Snowflake Cutout Cookies

Buddy's enthusiasm for Christmas whips through Walter's entire apartment, adorning every ceiling and counter with countless paper snowflakes. When you whisk cornstarch and confectioners' sugar into your sugar cookies, the classic recipe will transform, making cookies that are as light and airy as a flurry of snowflakes. And just like delicate snowflakes, this soft dough needs to stay cold to keep its shape. Work with a quarter of the dough at a time, keeping the rest cool in the refrigerator. The only melting should take place when these snowflake cookies reach your mouth!

MAKES 45 COOKIES

1 cup unsalted butter, chopped into $1/2$" cubes
$1\frac{1}{4}$ cups confectioners' sugar, divided
$1/2$ cup cornstarch
1 teaspoon vanilla extract
1 large egg
$1\frac{1}{2}$ cups all-purpose flour

1. In a large mixing bowl on low speed, add butter, then gradually add 1 cup confectioners' sugar and cornstarch until combined. Increase speed to medium and mix another 1 minute until pale.

2. With mixer still running on medium, add vanilla and egg. Sift in flour until mixed together.

3. Wrap dough in parchment paper and refrigerate 1 hour.

4. Preheat oven to 350°F.

5. Cut $1/4$ of dough and keep unused portion refrigerated. Roll out cut dough on a dusted surface to $1/4$" thickness.

6. Use a snowflake cookie cutter to cut out 11–12 shapes from dough and carefully transfer shapes to sheet lined with parchment paper, leaving $1/2$" between each.

7. Bake 10 minutes on lowest rack. Cookies will be pale in color but slightly firm to the touch when ready.

8. Dust cookies with remaining $1/4$ cup confectioners' sugar immediately, cool 5 minutes, then transfer to a cooling rack another 5 minutes.

9. Repeat cutting, rolling, shaping, and baking with remaining dough. Let cookies cool 2 hours before storing in an airtight container at room temperature, up to 3 days.

Tall Tales Trifle

Your friends and family will be amazed when you walk through the door with this show-stopping dessert, as visually fantastic as Buddy's tales of traveling through a candy cane forest and the Lincoln Tunnel. Stories are all about timing, and so is this trifle! Set the stage by baking the cake the night before. Keep the layers distinct by allowing the custard to cool completely before using it, and allow at least an hour for the cherry gelatin to set before the grand finale of whipped cream, cherries, and sprinkles.

SERVES 8

FOR MADEIRA CAKE
1 cup unsalted butter, room
    temperature
1 cup granulated sugar
4 large eggs, room temperature
1 teaspoon lemon zest
1 teaspoon vanilla extract
2 cups self-rising flour
1 tablespoon 2% milk

FOR CUSTARD
1 tablespoon unsalted butter
$3/4$ cup heavy cream
$1/2$ cup plain Greek yogurt
2 large eggs, room temperature
3 tablespoons cornstarch
$1/2$ cup granulated sugar
1 teaspoon vanilla extract

1. **To make Madeira Cake:** Preheat oven 350°F. Line a 9" square baking pan with parchment paper.

2. In a large bowl on medium speed, beat together butter and sugar 3 minutes until light in color. Add eggs, lemon zest, and vanilla and beat a further 30 seconds.

3. Sift in flour and mix on medium speed until combined. Add milk and mix a further 10 seconds.

4. Pour batter into pan and bake 1 hour until top is golden brown and a toothpick inserted into center comes out clean.

5. Let Cake cool in pan 20 minutes, then use a bread knife to cut into $1\frac{1}{2}$" cubes. Cover pan with a tea towel and refrigerate overnight.

6. **To make Custard:** In a medium saucepan over medium heat, combine butter, heavy cream, and yogurt. Warm $2\frac{1}{2}$ minutes, stirring occasionally.

7. In a measuring cup, add $1/4$ cup warm cream mixture. Whisk in eggs, cornstarch, and sugar until combined.

8. Pour egg mixture back into saucepan, reduce heat to low, and whisk constantly 5 minutes to thicken Custard.

9. Turn off heat and whisk in vanilla. Continue whisking 5 minutes.

continued

FOR ASSEMBLY

⅓ cup fresh lime juice

⅓ cup fresh orange juice

1 tablespoon gelatin powder

2 cups tart cherry juice

1 (24-ounce) jar pitted sour
   cherries, drained

1 (13-ounce) can whipped cream

7 maraschino cherries

¼ cup Hershey candy cane
   kisses

¼ cup gumdrop candies

¼ cup red, green, and white
   nonpareils

10. **To Assemble:** Layer Cake cubes into bottom of a trifle bowl. Drizzle lime juice and orange juice over Cake and let soak 5 minutes.

11. Pour Custard over Cake cubes. Use a spatula to smooth surface and to bring Custard up to sides of glass to create a seal. Place bowl in refrigerator 1 hour to set.

12. In a medium bowl, sprinkle gelatin powder over tart cherry juice and whisk with a fork. Let sit 1 minute, then microwave 1 minute (in 20-second intervals) on high, stirring between each interval.

13. Gently place sour cherries in an even layer on top of Custard, then carefully use a ladle to spoon cherry juice over cherries. Refrigerate at least 1½ hours to set, up to overnight.

14. Right before serving, pipe dollops of whipped cream neatly in a spiral from center of trifle bowl outward to edges. Create a second layer of whipped cream, starting 1" from edges of trifle bowl. Create a third layer 2" in from edge of bowl.

15. Top with maraschino cherries, candy cane kisses, gumdrops, and nonpareils before serving.

Plot Twist

Stories and recipes can both take an unexpected turn. If you've run out of time to prepare this dessert, simply improvise with premade pound cake and custard and use a 13-ounce jar of berry jam in place of the cherry gelatin.

CHAPTER 6

drinks

In the flurry of the season, sometimes a dash of extra Christmas joy is just what's needed to power up the mood. Your holiday spirit is bound to take flight when you share the following selection of drinks with your loved ones.

Set your season soaring with a round of Christmas Spirit Clausometers, a sip rich and decadent like fruitcake. And strike the right chord with your guests with a round of Central Park Caroling Coolers, featuring festive flavors of cherry and Cointreau. Looking for something every member of the family can enjoy? Each cocktail recipe in this chapter includes a mocktail version, so you can please elves of all sizes. You can also stir up nonalcoholic treats like a Mailroom Maple Fudge Mocha and Elf-ism Eggnog. Then, as the season winds down, raise a toast to a job well done with an Elves' Merrymaking Milk Shot. Cheers to a festive season celebrated right!

"World's Best Cup of Coffee"

Buddy's enthusiasm for all things Christmas is boundless, overflowing onto everyone and everything he meets. When you're brimming with excitement for gingerbread latte season, stir up a big batch of this simple recipe and add a splash of holiday enchantment to the lives of those around you. You can also make the brown sugar mixture ahead of time and refrigerate it to add to your usual cup of coffee whenever you please. Take a break from the daily grind to sip and savor the magic and wonder of the season.

SERVES 8

3/4 cup water
3/4 cup gently packed light brown sugar
2 tablespoons molasses
1/2 tablespoon ground cinnamon
1 teaspoon ground ginger
1/2 teaspoon ground black pepper
1/16 teaspoon ground cloves
1 teaspoon vanilla extract
1/2 teaspoon sea salt
5 cups black coffee
1 (13-ounce) can whipped cream
2 tablespoons edible gold stars

1. Put water, brown sugar, molasses, spices, vanilla, and salt in a small saucepan and stir over medium-low heat 5 minutes to dissolve sugar.

2. Remove from heat and cool 20 minutes.

3. To serve, pour 3 tablespoons into each mug, add coffee, stir, and garnish with whipped cream and gold stars.

4. Syrup can be stored by straining into a large, clean bottle and refrigerating up to 2 weeks.

Christmas Spirit Clausometers

When spirits are low, it's clear that a jump start of Christmas energy is needed. Rein your friends or family in for an impromptu gathering and dial up the festive vibes with this sweet, spirited concoction. To reignite that playful spark within you all, roll up a large batch of frosty ice cream snowballs beforehand to chill and set, and increase the amounts of the remaining ingredients so there are enough cocktails to go around. Before they leave, be sure to check your guests' Clausometers for safe takeoff!

SERVES 2

⅓ cup vanilla ice cream
2 ounces raspberry liqueur
2 ounces coconut liqueur
4 ounces sugar syrup, divided
2 ounces white crème de cacao
1 extra-large ice cube
¼ cup gold sanding sugar
2 (3") cinnamon sticks

1. Scoop vanilla ice cream into 2 balls and place onto a baking sheet lined with parchment paper. Freeze 1 hour.

2. In a cocktail shaker, add raspberry liqueur, coconut liqueur, 2 ounces sugar syrup, and white crème de cacao.

3. Add ice cube to shaker. Seal shaker and shake vigorously 30 seconds until cold and frosted. Set aside.

4. Pour remaining 2 ounces sugar syrup onto a small plate. Twist rims of two champagne coupe glasses into syrup. On another small plate, sprinkle gold sanding sugar and twist each glass rim in sugar.

5. Pour cocktail mixture into rimmed glasses. Add 1 scoop vanilla ice cream to each glass. Garnish each glass with a cinnamon stick.

Festive Fueled Frothometer

SERVES 2

2 cups vanilla ice cream
½ cup 2% milk
2 tablespoons grenadine
2 tablespoons coconut syrup
1 tablespoon white chocolate syrup
¼ teaspoon orange extract
1 teaspoon vanilla extract
⅛ teaspoon ground nutmeg

1. Scoop ice cream into a blender and pour in all remaining ingredients. Blend 30 seconds until smooth.
2. Divide milkshakes between two tall glasses and serve.

Passionfruit Spray Martinis

A fruity passionfruit perfume is not the sugary delight you might imagine. Luckily, you can craft a festive drink at home where there will be no confusion. Just remember to use fresh ginger, not ground ginger, as you shake things up. You want that first sip to be a delightful surprise, not a shock! For a magical addition, rim the martini glasses with a lime rind and mist a layer of edible glitter around the wet edges.

SERVES 2

2 large limes
2 ounces fresh passionfruit pulp
2 ounces pineapple juice
1 teaspoon fresh grated ginger
1 ounce grenadine
2 ounces vodka
1 large ice cube
Edible gold glitter spray
4 ounces sparkling wine

1. Use a citrus zester to peel long strips of lime rind to use as garnish. Set aside. Juice limes to squeeze out 2 ounces lime juice and add to a cocktail shaker. Reserve spent lime for rimming glasses.

2. Add remaining ingredients, excluding glittery spray and sparkling wine, to a cocktail shaker with ice cube.

3. Close lid and shake 30 seconds until container is cold to the touch and frosting on the outside.

4. Use discarded lime to rim two martini glasses, then spritz with gold glitter spray.

5. Strain the cocktail evenly between martini glasses, add 2 ounces sparkling wine to each glass, and stir. Garnish with a twist of lime rind.

Fresh Fruit Spray

SERVES 4

1 (4-ounce) can passionfruit pulp
1/4 cup fresh lime juice
1 teaspoon minced fresh ginger
1/2 cup fresh orange juice
2 cups soda water, chilled

1. In a large measuring cup, stir together the passionfruit pulp, lime juice, ginger, and orange juice.
2. Place in refrigerator and let mixture infuse 2 hours.
3. When ready to serve, strain 1/4 cup into each serving glass. Top each glass with 1/2 cup soda water.

Elves' Merrymaking Milk Shots

Even after Santa's big night is a wrap, the elves are just getting started on their own festive celebration. What better way to toast a job well done before beginning another round of preparations than with a creamy, sweet drink? The milk powder tastes like shortbread cookies once browned!

SERVES 2

¼ cup milk powder
⅓ cup coconut cream
6 tablespoons Marshmallow Fluff
4 ounces white crème de cacao
2 ounces gin
1 extra-large ice cube

1. Preheat oven to 300°F.

2. Evenly spread milk powder onto an unlined baking sheet. Bake 12 minutes, stirring halfway through. Set aside.

3. Scoop top layer of cream from coconut cream and combine with Marshmallow Fluff in a small saucepan. Stir over low heat 1 minute.

4. Remove from heat. Continue stirring another 1 minute until Marshmallow Fluff has completely dissolved.

5. Pour marshmallow mixture into a cocktail shaker along with white crème de cacao and gin. Add ice cube, then seal shaker. Shake vigorously 30 seconds until cold.

6. Moisten rims of two martini glasses with remaining coconut cream. Turn each glass upside down and twist it on plate of toasted milk powder to coat.

7. Strain between rimmed martini glasses and serve.

Faux Flurry

SERVES 1

1 cup coconut cream
6 tablespoons Marshmallow Fluff
2 ounces white chocolate syrup
1 ounce lemon syrup
1 extra-large ice cube
¼ cup toasted milk powder

1. Shake can of coconut cream and pour 1 cup into a small saucepan over low heat.
2. Stir in Marshmallow Fluff 2 minutes until dissolved.
3. Pour mixture into a cocktail shaker along with white chocolate syrup and lemon syrup. Add ice cube, then seal shaker. Shake vigorously 30 seconds until cold.
4. Rim two old-fashioned glassed following the same method as you would for the martini glass.
5. Strain mocktails evenly between prepared glasses and serve.

Central Park Caroling Coolers

With a simple carol, seasonal spirits and sleighs can soar. If you're feeling a bit out of tune with the season, strike the right chord by serving up this cocktail to help you set the Christmas mood not just for yourself but also for friends and family! The flavors are in perfect harmony, blending traditional Christmas notes of cherry and Cointreau. Before you know it, the entire gathering will be ready for another chorus of these drinks.

SERVES 2

8 cherries
2 ounces Cointreau
1 ounce tequila
4 ounces black cherry syrup
1 extra-large ice cube

1. Muddle cherries in a cocktail shaker using a spoon. Pour in Cointreau, tequila, and black cherry syrup.

2. Add extra-large ice cube and seal shaker. Shake vigorously 30 seconds until cold to the touch and frosted.

3. Strain cocktail into 2 champagne coupe glasses.

Melody Mocktail

SERVES 1

$1/8$ teaspoon ground ginger
$1/16$ teaspoon ground cardamom
1 whole star anise
$1/16$ teaspoon ground black pepper
1 tablespoon gently packed light brown sugar
$1/4$ cup orange juice
$1/2$ cup cherry juice
$1/2$ cup fizzy lemonade

1. Add ginger, cardamom, star anise, black pepper, and brown sugar to orange juice in a small cup and microwave 15 seconds to heat gently. Stir to dissolve sugar.

2. Discard star anise and pour mixture into a highball glass. Top with cherry juice and fizzy lemonade and stir.

Mailroom Maple Fudge Mochas

Buddy knows that maple syrup sweetens everything up, even in the trenches of the daily grind. Start your day with a little extra shine by swirling some maple fudge syrup into a mocha and sucking it back to make little moments wonderful again. Generously share the sweet scoops of maple fudge in mugs of coffee with your own buddies for merry memories. You can also gift bottles of the syrup mixture with bags of your favorite coffee. After all, sharing is what the holidays are all about!

SERVES 12

3/4 cup maple syrup, divided
1/2 cup granulated sugar
1/4 cup unsalted butter
1 cup heavy cream
1 teaspoon sea salt
1/2 cup white chocolate chips
1 teaspoon vanilla extract
5 cups black coffee
1 (13-ounce) can whipped cream

1. In a medium saucepan over medium heat, add 1/2 cup maple syrup, sugar, butter, heavy cream, and salt. Stir 5 minutes until sugar dissolves.

2. Reduce heat to medium-low and let simmer 30 minutes, stirring occasionally.

3. Stir in white chocolate chips until dissolved.

4. Turn off heat and mix in vanilla.

5. Spoon 2 tablespoons maple mixture into each of twelve Irish coffee mugs. Top with black coffee and stir until dissolved. Top with whipped cream 1 1/2" high and drizzle 1 teaspoon maple syrup on top of each mug.

Smoother Shot

While Buddy knows maple syrup is good with everything, his new friend in the mailroom knows a shot of a little something makes the day go smoother. If you want to be generous to the adults on Christmas morning, add a shot of Baileys Irish Cream to each mug. That'll really kick things off!

Gnomes' Secret Glühwein

Elves may excel at toymaking, but gnomes seem to have stumbled on a good thing of their own! Some may consider taste-testing this German mulled wine part of the job, but when you make this recipe at home, you can savor every sip. Glühwein can also be made in advance to have on hand for impromptu gatherings. Once cooked, allow to cool to room temperature before straining into a glass jug. Store in the refrigerator up to 3 days. When ready to serve, rewarm the glühwein on the stove over medium-low heat.

SERVES 5

1 (750-milliliter) bottle dry red wine
1/2 cup water
1 cup brandy
3/4 cup granulated sugar
1 (3") cinnamon stick
6 whole cloves
12 whole black peppercorns
1 large lemon, zested and juiced
2 large navel oranges, zested and juiced
1 large Granny Smith apple, cored and chopped

1. In a large saucepan over medium heat, pour in red wine, water, brandy, and sugar. Stir and cook 5 minutes until sugar has dissolved.

2. Add cinnamon stick, cloves, peppercorns, lemon zest and juice, orange zest and juice, and apple and stir. Reduce heat to medium-low and let steep 30 minutes.

3. Strain into five Irish coffee mugs and serve.

The Spontaneous Seasonal Sip

SERVES 6

3 cups cranberry juice
3 cups apple juice
3/4 cup granulated sugar
1 (3") cinnamon stick
6 whole cloves
12 whole black peppercorns
1 large lemon, zested and juiced
2 large navel oranges, zested and juiced
1 large Granny Smith apple, cored and chopped

1. In a large saucepan over medium heat, pour in cranberry juice, apple juice, and sugar. Stir and cook 5 minutes until sugar has dissolved.

2. Add cinnamon stick, cloves, peppercorns, lemon zest and juice, orange zest and juice, and apple and stir. Reduce heat to low-medium and let steep 15 minutes. Turn off heat and let sit for a further 15 minutes before straining into six Irish coffee mugs and serving.

Cola Chugger

In one astonishing gulp, Buddy downs an entire two-liter bottle of soda. And when the fizz is this fabulous, why would you want to stop? Keep this recipe fresh by mixing up a larger batch of cherry juice, grenadine, lime juice, and bitters earlier in the day. When it's time to tingle taste buds, pour one-quarter cup of the mixture into a glass and top with three-quarters cup cola. Friends and family will be eager for more.

SERVES 1

¼ cup tart cherry juice
1 tablespoon grenadine
1 tablespoon fresh lime juice
3 drops bitters
¾ cup cola

In a highball glass, combine tart cherry juice, grenadine, lime juice, bitters, and cola. Add 3 ice cubes and serve.

Swirly Twirly Gumdrops

Fantastical stories swirl around Buddy wherever he goes! Just as colorful as his adventures, this cocktail pops with fruity flavors while gumdrops playfully bob above frothy waves of foam. There's no need to hitch a sleighride to the North Pole to create this magic! Be sure to shake the egg whites in your shaker without ice; otherwise, it'll struggle to froth up. And once the gumdrops are skewered across the surface, these tasty drinks will be ready to set sail to friends around you.

SERVES 2

2 ounces fresh orange juice
1 1/2 teaspoons citric acid
1 ounce peach schnapps
1 ounce grenadine
2 large egg whites, room temperature
1 extra-large ice cube
2 ounces sparkling water
6 gumdrop candies

1. In a small cup, microwave orange juice 20 seconds, just until warm. Stir in citric acid until fully dissolved.

2. In a cocktail shaker, add orange juice mixture, peach schnapps, grenadine, and egg whites. Seal shaker and shake vigorously without ice for 30 seconds to create foam.

3. Add ice cube to shaker, then seal again. Shake another 20 seconds to chill.

4. Strain cocktail evenly into two martini glasses. Use a spoon handle to create a small opening in foam and pour in sparkling water. Stir gently to combine but not enough to disrupt foam.

5. Thread 3 gumdrop candies each onto two cocktail skewers. Place a skewer over rim of each cocktail glass to garnish.

Gumdrops Galore

SERVES 1

1/2 cup fresh orange juice
1/2 teaspoon citric acid
1/4 cup peach nectar
1 ounce grenadine
3/4 cup sparkling water
3 gumdrop candies

1. In a small cup, microwave orange juice 20 seconds to warm, then stir in citric acid until dissolved.

2. Pour into a highball glass and stir in peach nectar, grenadine, and sparkling water until combined. Top with crushed ice.

3. Skewer 3 gumdrops onto a cocktail skewer, and place over rim of glass to garnish.

Snow Globe Spritzes

The Empire State Building glistens in the palm of Buddy's hand as he navigates to find his family. When you make the family rounds yourself, be sure to have this drink in hand. A festive flurry of coconut and peppermint flavors swirl with edible dust around an ice "globe." Just a gentle whirl will bring the glittery concoction to life!

SERVES 4

1 cup boiled filtered water
4 (2") rosemary sprigs
¼ cup sugar syrup
¼ cup white sparkling sugar
4 cups sparkling lemonade
4 ounces coconut syrup
1 teaspoon peppermint extract
¼ teaspoon silver edible pearl
  dust

1. Make ice globes the night before by boiling filtered water in a tea kettle.

2. Allow water to cool for 1 hour before pouring into extra-large silicone ice ball trays. Press a rosemary sprig through pour hole of silicone tray and freeze 6 hours, up to overnight.

3. Pour sugar syrup onto a small plate and twist rims of four old-fashioned glasses to coat.

4. Pour white sparkling sugar onto a second small plate and twist glass rims into sugar to coat.

5. Pour sparkling lemonade, coconut syrup, peppermint extract, and silver edible pearl dust into glasses and stir. Place 1 large ice cube sphere gently in each glass and serve.

Elf-ism Eggnog

There are a lot of things you may not know about elves, but one thing is for sure: their playful spirit means they've mastered the art of infusing magic into the mundane. Some skills, like becoming Master Tinker, take time, but that playful spirit won't take long to re-create with this simple, tasty drink. Colorful marshmallows and a fun swirl of whipped cream atop traditional eggnog show just what it means to be an elf.

SERVES 4

1 1/2 cups 2% milk
1 1/2 cups heavy cream
6 large egg yolks
1/2 cup granulated sugar
1/8 teaspoon ground nutmeg
2 ounces rum extract or imitation rum extract
1 (13-ounce) can whipped cream
1/4 cup mini multicolored marshmallows
20 pieces candy corn

1. Heat milk and heavy cream in a small saucepan over low heat 3 minutes until warm but not hot.
2. Whisk together egg yolks, sugar, and nutmeg in a large measuring cup.
3. Gradually add 1/4 cup warmed milk mixture to egg yolk mixture, constantly whisking to temper eggs.
4. Pour egg yolk mixture back into saucepan with remaining milk mixture. Cook over low heat, constantly whisking, 7–8 minutes until mixture is steaming but not boiling. If mixture begins to overheat, remove it from heat and whisk in cold milk until it cools slightly. Stir in rum extract.
5. Pour into four Irish coffee mugs and top with whipped cream, marshmallows, and candy corn. Serve.

Sticky Sidewalks

Buddy may have been warned to keep his sticky paws off any "candy" on the street, but this is a treat you won't need to leave alone. Served in a glass decorated to mimic the look of sticky gum, no one will be able to help sneaking a taste of this cocktail! Real gum might effortlessly cling to any surface, but for this drink, a piping bag becomes a handy tool. Paint your glasses in shades of bubble gum pink, or switch out the food coloring to playful purples, piping the icing in squiggly, gooey designs along the rim. As everyone gets stuck into their drink, toast to life's sweet moments together.

SERVES 2

FOR MARTINI GLASS RIM
3 tablespoons confectioners' sugar
1/4 teaspoon rose pink food coloring
1/2 teaspoon water

FOR STICKY SIDEWALKS
2 ounces green sour apple syrup
1 ounce pink lemonade concentrate
2 ounces vodka
1 ounce strawberry liqueur
1/4 teaspoon vanilla extract
1 extra-large ice cube
2 ounces sparkling water

1. **To prepare Martini Glass Rim:** Stir confectioners' sugar, rose pink food coloring, and water together in a small bowl to form a thick paste. Spoon into a piping bag and pipe onto rims of two martini glasses. Let set 30 minutes.

2. **To make Sticky Sidewalks:** In a cocktail shaker, combine sour apple syrup, pink lemonade concentrate, vodka, strawberry liqueur, and vanilla. Add an extra-large ice cube. Shake vigorously 20 seconds until shaker feels cold.

3. Strain into prepared martini glasses and top with sparkling water. Stir and serve.

Gummy Gulper

SERVES 1

FOR HURRICANE GLASS RIM
3 tablespoons confectioners' sugar
1/4 teaspoon rose pink food coloring
1/2 teaspoon water

FOR GUMMY GULPER
3 ounces sour apple syrup
1 1/2 ounces pink lemonade concentrate
1 1/2 teaspoons vanilla extract
1 1/2 ounces strawberry syrup
1 1/4 cups sparkling water

1. Rim a hurricane glass following the same method as you would for the martini glass.
2. Stir together sour apple syrup, pink lemonade concentrate, vanilla, strawberry syrup, and sparkling water in glass. Top with crushed ice and serve.

Old Saint Nick

A chaotic night can have even Santa feeling as though he's too old for this. If you lose your own momentum as you gear up for the most magical time of the year, the Christmas Spiced Sugar Cubes in this recipe can transform any drink, from the old-fashioned cocktail here to a cup of tea or hot chocolate. Just like magic, with each sip, you'll be reminded that the joy of the season knows no age and spirits will soar once again.

For Christmas Spiced Sugar Cubes

MAKES 16

¾ cup granulated sugar
½ teaspoon ground allspice
¼ teaspoon ground cloves
1 teaspoon ground cinnamon
½ tablespoon water
¼ teaspoon orange extract

For Old Saint Nick

SERVES 1

1 Christmas Spiced Sugar Cube
3 dashes (about ⅛ teaspoon) bitters
1 (3"-strip) orange peel
1 maraschino cherry
1 teaspoon fresh orange juice
1 ounce Scotch whiskey
1 extra-large ice cube

1. **To make Christmas Spiced Sugar Cubes:** In a small bowl, mix sugar, allspice, cloves, and cinnamon until spices are evenly distributed through sugar.

2. Add water and stir until sugar is damp but not wet. Mixture will look crumbly yet moist. Sprinkle orange extract over sugar mixture and stir to combine.

3. Fill 16 (1") compartments of an ice cube tray with mixture, pressing sugar down firmly. Let dry 8 hours, then remove from tray and store in an airtight container at room temperature 3 months.

4. **To make Old Saint Nick:** Place Sugar Cube into an old-fashioned glass and drop bitters over Sugar Cube.

5. Add orange peel and cherry and use a spoon to muddle ingredients together. Add orange juice and whiskey.

6. Add ice cube and let sit 10 minutes to chill whiskey. Let ice begin to melt before serving.

Jolly Saint Nick

SERVES 1

2 Christmas Spiced Sugar Cubes
1 maraschino cherry
½ cup fresh orange juice
½ cup ginger ale
1 teaspoon fresh lemon juice

Muddle Sugar Cubes with maraschino cherry in an old-fashioned glass. Top with orange juice, ginger ale, and lemon juice. Stir and serve.

STANDARD US/METRIC
MEASUREMENT CONVERSIONS

VOLUME CONVERSIONS

US Volume Measure	Metric Equivalent
⅛ teaspoon	0.5 milliliter
¼ teaspoon	1 milliliter
½ teaspoon	2 milliliters
1 teaspoon	5 milliliters
½ tablespoon	7 milliliters
1 tablespoon (3 teaspoons)	15 milliliters
2 tablespoons (1 fluid ounce)	30 milliliters
¼ cup (4 tablespoons)	60 milliliters
⅓ cup	90 milliliters
½ cup (4 fluid ounces)	125 milliliters
⅔ cup	160 milliliters
¾ cup (6 fluid ounces)	180 milliliters
1 cup (16 tablespoons)	250 milliliters
1 pint (2 cups)	500 milliliters
1 quart (4 cups)	1 liter (about)

WEIGHT CONVERSIONS

US Weight Measure	Metric Equivalent
½ ounce	15 grams
1 ounce	30 grams
2 ounces	60 grams
3 ounces	85 grams
¼ pound (4 ounces)	115 grams
½ pound (8 ounces)	225 grams
¾ pound (12 ounces)	340 grams
1 pound (16 ounces)	454 grams

OVEN TEMPERATURE CONVERSIONS

Degrees Fahrenheit	Degrees Celsius
200 degrees F	95 degrees C
250 degrees F	120 degrees C
275 degrees F	135 degrees C
300 degrees F	150 degrees C
325 degrees F	160 degrees C
350 degrees F	180 degrees C
375 degrees F	190 degrees C
400 degrees F	205 degrees C
425 degrees F	220 degrees C
450 degrees F	230 degrees C

BAKING PAN SIZES

American	Metric
8 × 1½ inch round baking pan	20 × 4 cm cake tin
9 × 1½ inch round baking pan	23 × 3.5 cm cake tin
11 × 7 × 1½ inch baking pan	28 × 18 × 4 cm baking tin
13 × 9 × 2 inch baking pan	30 × 20 × 5 cm baking tin
2 quart rectangular baking dish	30 × 20 × 3 cm baking tin
15 × 10 × 2 inch baking pan	30 × 25 × 2 cm baking tin (Swiss roll tin)
9 inch pie plate	22 × 4 or 23 × 4 cm pie plate
7 or 8 inch springform pan	18 or 20 cm springform or loose bottom cake tin
9 × 5 × 3 inch loaf pan	23 × 13 × 7 cm or 2 lb narrow loaf or pate tin
1½ quart casserole	1.5 liter casserole
2 quart casserole	2 liter casserole

index

about the author

Bryton Taylor is the creator of InLiterature.net and PopcornPairings.com, food blogs where she creates authentic recipes inspired by your favorite novels and movies, and the author of *The Unofficial Home Alone Cookbook*. Best known for her *YouTube* videos, Bryt can be found whipping up exquisite sweet treats like Turkish Delight inspired by *The Lion, the Witch and the Wardrobe* or concocting delicious magical potions that transport you to Alice's Wonderland. Whether you're inviting friends over for a movie night or planning your next book club get-together, Bryt helps you re-create food items just as they'd appear in your favorite books and movies to make an unforgettable experience for lasting memories.